Tie

1958

THE NAKED GOD

THE NAKED GOD

THE WRITER AND THE COMMUNIST PARTY

By HOWARD FAST

FREDERICK A. PRAEGER, *Publisher*

NEW YORK, N. Y.

BOOKS THAT MATTER

First published in the United States
of America, 1957

by Frederick A. Praeger, Inc.,
15 West 47 Street, New York 36

Library of Congress Catalog Card Number 57-14824

Printed in the United States of America

Freedom for supporters of the government only, for the members of one party only—no matter how big its membership may be—is no freedom at all. Freedom is always freedom for the man who thinks differently. This contention does not spring from a fanatical love of abstract "justice," but from the fact that everything which is enlightening, healthy and purifying in political freedom derives from its independent character, and from the fact that freedom loses all its virtue when it becomes a privilege. . . .

The suppression of political life throughout the country must gradually cause the vitality of the Soviets themselves to decline. Without general elections, freedom of the press, freedom of assembly, and freedom of speech, life in every public institution slows down, becomes a caricature of itself, and bureaucracy rises as the only deciding factor. No one can escape the workings of this law. . . .

—Rosa Luxemburg, 1918, in "Die Russische Revolution"

THE NAKED GOD

1

Where do I begin? Such stories have no ending until you, yourself, end—and even then the threads are picked up by others to be unraveled to a source that is somehow always over the horizon. As I go back in my memories, there is place after place—and yet always one returns to the innocent wisdom of Lewis Carroll, who said that all stories should begin at the beginning.

I had a god who walked naked, but nobody among those I loved said so; for even as the innocent wisdom of Hans Christian Andersen held that those who could not see the king's clothes were persons of small intellect and unfit for the positions they held, so in my world, it was the conviction of millions of good and wise folk that only those who had lost all honor, dignity, decency and courage would dare to point out that this god whom we worshiped for his noble raiment was indeed naked and ugly in his nakedness.

Who would be without honor, dignity, decency and courage?

In the little town where I live, there is a little store, unimportant and of no consequence, and out of this store an old man ekes a living. This is an old man who mourns a hurt which will not heal, the kind of a hurt many who read this will know intimately, for twenty years ago the young son of this man fell in Spain, fighting in the Lincoln Battalion for the Spanish Republic and the freedom of men.

His son lies buried in the distant Spanish soil, and for twenty years the hurt in this old man was as if it had happened yesterday.

He had a little salve to rub on the terrible sore. This was the salve, that his son had died in the best of causes, the fight for the liberation of mankind. But in 1956, a man called Khrushchev delivered a certain "secret report"—telling a story of Russia and the Communist movement that I and my friends had heard before but had never believed before. Now Khrushchev made proof of twenty-five years of "slander," and we believed. And among those who believed because they had to believe was this old man whose son had laid down his life in Spain.

I came into his store one day in that month of June and he was weeping. He asked me,

"Why did my son die?"

For had I not held, all of my thinking life and in all that I wrote, that one son of man was all the sons of man? He then said to me, but not in words—for a broken heart does not make a gentle person cruel or vindictive—not in words but with the look in his eyes,

"That I, a plain man did not comprehend this is no wonder; but you, Howard Fast, spoke and wrote and pleaded this cause—and why? Can you tell me why?"

But I don't know if I can answer that. I want a beginning, a nodule point to make it plain and evident, and then I can go ahead to write down, to the best of my ability and understanding, an explanation of why, when the god was naked, we told ourselves and the whole world that he was quite otherwise.

But so complex, so troubled, so filled with passion, incident and outcry is my own past; and so much more complex the world's past in which my own tiny effort was made, that I find it almost impossible to place brick upon brick, as a good builder or writer should—making an orderly procession of thoughts, ideas and conclusions.

Nor have I been able, in the year or so that has gone by since the remnants of my long structure of belief crumbled into ashes, to create any theoretical apology. Of such apology I have read at least half a million words, from the simple and insolent idiocy of the men in the Kremlin who explain a river of blood and anguish by saying, "cult of the individual," to the finely wrought and beautifully written phrases of Hyman Levy, the British Marxist.

Such apology—all of it that I have read—has less intrinsic meaning for me than the picture of a single tear of an innocent man who is being tortured to confess to crimes he never committed or dreamed of. For twenty and more years of my life, I created for myself a world picture based on the theory of those who pleased to call themselves "Marxists." I came finally to understand the stern injunction of Karl Marx, when he declared, "I am no Marxist!"

Theory, where it is not worthless, is a part of science and the scientific method. But if we are to explain and understand a little of the godhood of communism, we must begin by understanding that we are not dealing with social science or any other kind of scientific movement and outlook; we are dealing with naked terror, awful brutality, and frightening ignorance.

We are also dealing with an epoch, with great movements and struggles of men and of nations; but movements of such size tend to become meaningless and impersonal.

This does not entice me. I am neither impersonal nor objective; I write of what I have lived and been, and I cannot write without anger and shame and hatred. For it is not myself alone who has been degraded, but a whole generation of brave and eager youth—men and women who set out to scale the very ramparts of heaven, and then, reaching the top, look over and down into the ugliness of hell.

It can only be fully meaningful if one makes the same journey—and then sees what a single Communist saw. No theory, no historical objectivity can substitute for this.

Comrade Kedrov saw this. When he lived, breathed, dreamed, struggled and climbed those ramparts of heaven, I knew him not; nor can I find any material that will give him form, shape, age or character. I found his name only after he was dead, only after he lay prone on those ramparts, looking into the face of hell, and scratched out his last plea to the naked god. I learned about him when Khrushchev told his story to the Twentieth Congress of the Communist Party of the Soviet Union. Here, according to Khrushchev, is what Comrade Kedrov wrote as he lay dying in a Soviet prison:

"Everything, however, has its limits. My torture has reached the extreme. My health is broken, my strength and my energy are waning, the end is drawing near. To die in a Soviet prison, branded as a vile traitor to the Fatherland— what can be more monstrous for an honest man? And how monstrous all this is! Unsurpassed bitterness and pain grips my heart. . . ."

Is this then, the beginning and the end? As man finally, in his own good time, puts aside all tyrannies, so will there be an end of the Communist movement as we know it. What then? Will the world comprehend Comrade Kedrov? Will a monument be raised to him? Will some Russian novelist, freed finally of his soul's enthrallment, write the whole story of Comrade Kedrov's torment? Or will he be forgotten?

But can he be forgotten? Has he not, in his few words, given me a whole text? He says what only a Communist can say, for only the Communist has paid the price for saying it:

"How monstrous all this is!"

He has lived and died in the paradox of our time, a part of one of the greatest, most violent and awful dramas in all the history of mankind. Yet the paradox itself is a part of the reality. Comrade Kedrov was not tricked, taken in by some unholy deception—any more than I and my own comrades were tricked or taken in by deception. Pledged to the pure light of reason, Comrade Kedrov was destroyed by unreason—but he played a part in the making of the unreason.

It can be said best in the language of literature, better than in the language of politics. Man had suffered too much, hungered too much—and the future was too distant. He agreed not to wait; he would carry his objective in a single, final storm—and the storm consumed him.

Yet such was his dedication to his brief vision of utopia that he lost sight of himself—and thereby of all mankind. So well was it put by John Donne—that "No man is an island, entire of itself"; and Sartre, who lived and grew in fire, spelled out a philosophy of the responsibility of man to himself. Always new, this is also very ancient, more ancient by far than Shakespeare's instruction, "To thine own self be true . . ."

There was the evil in what we dreamed of as Communists; we took the noblest dreams and hopes of mankind as

our credo; the evil we did was to accept the degradation of
our own souls—and because we surrendered in ourselves, in
our own Party existence, all the best and most precious gains
and liberties of mankind—because we did this, we betrayed
mankind, and the Communist Party became a thing of destruction.

Yet I wonder whether Comrade Kedrov understood this
ever—even at that final moment when he was dragged from
his prison cell to be put to death by the firing squad. At
the very end, he wrote,

"Neither the Party, nor the Soviet government . . . will
permit this cruel, irreparable injustice."

How wrong he was! He had lost his most precious possession—the knowledge that his suffering was all suffering,
and therefore he could not comprehend that it was the Party
that tortured him—the Party that had reached the point of
destruction.

There wase no Soviet government; there is none today.
The people of the Soviet Union live and die as the Party
dictates. The Comrade Kedrovs, in the uncounted tens of
thousands, are dead.

Yet for Comrade Kedrov there will be a monument—
even as there must be a memory and a monument for every
human being struck down by a tyrant's blow. His story will
be remembered here, in what follows—and it will also be
remembered in the documents that thousands of other Communists will write—until the world learns, out of its own
deep agony, that the dignity of one man, any man, is in a
very true way, the dignity of all men.

2

I joined the Communist Party in 1943, but I came to it first as a part of my generation, in the 1930's. In 1932, I worked as a messenger in a Harlem Branch of the New York Public Library. It was one of a series of dismal and underpaid jobs that I had held since, at the age of eleven, pressed by the need of our utter poverty, I went to work as a newspaper delivery boy. The fact that thereby I gave up all the joy and laughter of childhood to embark upon long years of physical and mental weariness—the particular weariness of doomed children that Jack London has described so well—is important only in its very broad social sense.

If we are to seek for understanding, any sort of understanding, through this document, then the reader must not only recall the 1930's, but must comprehend the full meaning of the surrender of childhood, a situation that poverty still imposes on millions of children the world over. The fact that I earned twenty-five cents an hour at this job is of less moment, for my twenty-five cents was precious beyond belief, and when I bought apples from one or another of the thousands of much older men who had lost all the gain and security of a lifetime, I felt keenly my own fortune as against their total tragedy. I was lucky. I always found work and a few dollars, whether in a factory at forty cents an hour or shoveling snow or heaving rocks or doing errands.

I was large and strong, iron-muscled, youthfully indestructible, for I had already survived and made my peace with every bestiality and indignity that poverty exacts. I was the product of the gutter and the gang, the lousy, bedbug-ridden railroad tenement, the burning streets and the empty lots. I had carried brass knucks and used them, and in my animal world, I was beaten and I beat others. I had no mother to account to—she had died years before—and my father was an industrial worker, unemployed for months at a time, aging, his back broken with years as an ironworker, tinworker, cable-car conductor and garment worker.

My childhood friends are with me no more. A few survived in soul as well as body, but others found their fate in the electric chair, in the skid rows of alcoholism, in prison and in other bitter places. To this day, I cannot pass a begger, a broken man, a homeless wretch crouched on some sidewalk without saying to myself,

"There—but by the grace of God."

I do not try to account for my own fortune. At an age earlier than I can remember I found a passion and love that was to remain with me all my life; I entered the world of books. I read everything; and thereby perhaps, found my own salvation. I read, not with taste, discrimination or selectivity, but with simple and direct lust. A book was a book, and I passed no more judgment than a thirsty man would pass upon water.

Years later, during World War II, I sprawled on the floor of a C-46 that was flying from Casablanca to Bengasi. We had a bad motor, turbulent air and electric storm, and as the plane tossed and shook, our little group of army personnel lay quietly, caught in the fear of any group of Americans who faced coming down in the desert in those days. Only one man in the plane was unafraid, and that was because he was unaware; his soul had taken wings, and for him they were surer wings than our plane carried. It was nighttime, and the plane was in blackout darkness. Only one tiny blue light burned in the ceiling of the cargo hold where we lay. This man I speak of—he was a boy of eighteen—clung with one hand to the cargo rail that runs along the ceiling of a C-46; with the other hand, he held a book, one of those paper-covered armed-service editions, up to the tiny blue light. Only the story in the book existed for him, nothing else; and all through the flight, he hung there in that uncomfortable position, reading.

When we finally landed, I sought him out, to find out what book had so enthralled him. But the book—a light little thing called *Lady into Fox*—was not important in terms of its content, but only as a book. The boy came from a tiny village in Tennessee; he was literate yet illiterate, and not until he went into the army had he ever read a book. Then a world opened. The war ceased to exist; the army ceased to exist; he had entered the world of books. I tried to find out what kind of books he liked, but the question had no meaning for him. He loved books—all books.

So it was with me during those years when life was work, poverty and hunger. I read through the fiction shelves of the Public Library from A to Z. I read non-fiction, subject after subject, row upon row of books. Little enough of what I read was I able to comprehend or correlate, but I knew only that I bathed in the whole great, beautiful, complicated and glorious world that was hidden from my own limited eyes.

Long afterward, when Alexander Woollcott discovered my book, *The Last Frontier,* and had it accepted by the

Reader's Club—he was one of the board of judges—I met that grand, irascible and acid-tongued man himself. He was bewailing the fact that no one in our whole land even knew, much less read, such worthy writers as Anthony Trollope, and when I demurred that I had, he bluntly called me a liar.

"What Trollope have you read?" he demanded. "And why?"

I could only remember *The Warden* and *Barchester Towers,* and as to why—well, I explained that Trollope was in the Ts. But so it was, and sometimes I ask myself, when was there a time in my conscious life that I did not want to be a writer?

In this library where I worked in 1932, there was a gentle and wise librarian who was willing to read stories I had written and to say something about them—in particular to wonder where, in my writing, was my own life and experience. I explained that I did not consider my life and experience fit subjects for anything but forgetfulness—which was why I preferred to try to write like Cabell or Robert Louis Stevenson. My own life was meaningless, senseless, hopeless, degraded and without direction. Who would write of such things?

Whereupon she showed me, for the first time, the writing of Communists—and then, when suddenly a vision of sanity and order and hope burst upon me, she gave me Shaw's wonderful book to read, *The Intelligent Woman's Guide to Socialism and Capitalism.* I read it through in one night—and then Shaw was my idol and teacher forever afterward.

Now I do not hold that you or anyone else today will become a convert to socialism by reading this book of Shaw's;

but today is not 1932—and you are not me; and you do not see now, as I saw then, as I drifted through America, the kids like myself clinging to the boxcars, journeying here and there, from nowhere to nowhere—in search of hope. But you must comprehend this if you are to comprehend anything of the strange paradox of communism and the Communist Party in our time.

I did not join the Communist Party then. My battle for my own salvation as an individual bulked too large. There were, unfortunately, only twenty-four hours in a day, and a minimum number of hours were needed for sleep and work—work that I had to do to live. That left hardly enough for writing and learning, and either I would become a professional writer or I would die in the attempt. Yet I became aware of the Party and the American Left. I went to meetings of the John Reed Club and came away with anger and mistrust, for I had never known intellectuals, and I could comprehend neither the speech nor the people. I had to become aware that my own gutter language was perhaps not the manner of my time, that words written in books were also spoken by certain people, and that there was a world where battle was with ideas rather than fists. I learned a great deal.

And through the years, on and off, the Party always rubbed against the edge of my life—even as it did with millions the world over. I made friends who were Communists, argued with them, fought with them, bought the *Daily Worker*, sneered at it, read it hungrily, sneered at it again. In 1939, when the pact between Hitler Germany and Soviet Russia was signed, my wife and I broke with our Communist friends in a bitter climax of growing resentment. I had become an anti-Fascist. My whole thinking existence was dedicated to the proposition that Hitlerism and civilization were incompatible. I had not been born into civilization; civilization and culture, art and literature—these were man's gifts to me; they were my life, my existence—the blood and tissue of my own resurrection. I lived, even as so many of my generation lived, that fascism might perish.

In that time when England stood alone against the monster, my heart went out to her. My England was not only the London of my long dead mother's stories of her girlhood, not simply the golden land of the literature and language that had become my work in life; but also the land of Shelley and of the songs of Shelley—who sang of liberty as no other did. England was St. George against the dragon of hate and horror that Hitler and Nazism had created. To me—and I have no doubt that I see most things too simply, too much in blacks and whites—it was England for mankind. Whereby, I not only broke with those Communists I knew, but I looked upon them with contempt and anger.

Yet four years later, I joined the Communist Party— not because I ever changed my judgment on the pact, not because I could ever forgive it or pardon it, which my friends in the Party knew—but because when I, in my whole body and being, became a part of that terrible moment in history which we call World War II, I came to accept the proposition that the truest and most consistent fighters in this anti-Fascist struggle were the Communists.

I had watched many other writers join the Communist Party and then leave it in bitterness and disillusionment. I had witnessed their affection for the Party turning into hatred. I had read their testimony. Yet I was able to tell myself that this was the past—and that I must make my own decision out of the present. For good or for bad, I always arrived at the end point of decision as my own responsibility —and now too.

Yet I joined as a writer, even as so many other writers of our epoch had joined. Perhaps no other group of human beings who earn their bread with a skill or a trade have so deep and pressing a need to understand the movements and compulsions of both history and the individual as the creative writer. Perhaps no other have so pressing a need to resolve out of man's agony and joy, a goal, a reason, a pattern of sense—for these are the working tools of the writer. It is the particular curse of the writer, as I must repeat over and over, that freedom, a luxury to some others, is a necessity to him; for without freedom, he cannot grow or develop— and perhaps it is also his grace.

So, in 1943, I saw the Communists as the bravest and most skillful fighters for man's freedom. I was mistaken. But a conviction thus arrived at is not easily undone.

3

Later on in this book, I will tell in a good deal of detail of the method whereby the Communist Party *must* destroy the independence, the skill and the talent of the artists who become part of it. That this is not the most important of what the Party destroys goes without saying, yet if the writer is not the focal point of the storm and the awful destruction visited by the storm, he is nevertheless a very true barometer. Even as in the modern epoch, one can fairly well pass judgment upon a society by its attitude toward the Jews within it and toward anti-Semitism, so throughout history, the attitude toward the writer was almost definitive in indicating the social health of the society itself.

For the moment, I feel that I must continue and complete this brief personal history which is a not unimportant prelude to the substance of my argument.

If any reader imagines that out of the act of joining the Communist Party there comes either internal peace or happiness, he is mistaken. In all truth, one sells his soul, accepting the proposition that thus will mankind be redeemed—and with it the circumstances of such a process of redemption, that therein neither individual indignity nor hurt is of any importance. The similes of the Party—and it has many, since they offer a convenient substitute for thought—are neither colorful nor inspiring, for they emerge from the dreariness of the whole. One of these is to the effect that a person comes into the Party carrying "bourgeois baggage," of which he must divest himself. The pride, passion and independence of the individual are described as this "baggage," and it becomes an important, if not the most important, admission of a lack of "proletarianism" to admit to them. My entire background of the working class, of poverty and hunger, did not help to make me "proletarian." Only the ignominious retreat of my spirit could prove my faith.

It is quite impossible for me to attempt any detailed exposition of this process during the years between 1943, when I entered the Party, and 1957, when I made public announcement of the fact that I had left it.

It is quite true that, unlike Comrade Kedrov and a hundred thousand others in those lands where the Communist Party holds power, I never had to submit to torture or confinement in a prison cell or the firing squad as recognition on the part of my leaders. But this lamentable lack of governmental authority only called for more adroitness and delicacy on their parts. Even if the body is protected by law, the spirit can still be hammered into shape; and it would require many long volumes to spell out the process. Nor would such listings make pleasant reading for any sane person.

The manner is more important than the quantity, and the manner can be explained. In 1945, I took ship in Calcutta to return to the United States. Before leaving India, I had a long talk with one of the top leaders of the Communist Party of India. He spoke to me as a newspaperman but also as a Communist, and he told me of his feeling that, after the war, Great Britain would be forced to relinquish her hold on India. He made several points with great em-

phasis, and he begged me to convey his opinions to Eugene
Dennis, then general secretary of the Communist Party of
the United States. He said that he felt it was of the utmost
importance that the Communist Party in the United States
be informed of these pending developments in India.

The substance of his analysis is of no great importance
today, since history has ridden roughshod over it. To satisfy
the curiosity of those who may wonder, I will say that he was
wrong in every prediction except that of independence—and
even on the manner in which independence for India would
be achieved, he was also wrong.

But I did not know this in 1945. I only knew that he
felt his thinking to be of paramount importance and wished
it to be conveyed to Dennis, and this I took very seriously.
The day I arrived home, I tried to make an appointment
to see Dennis.

But he was too busy. I had come fifteen thousand miles
from a theatre of war and could try to reach him the first
day I was home with my family; but he was too busy. The
days stretched into weeks, and I pleaded and opportuned,
but Dennis was too busy. Finally he found a moment for me.

I went down to 12th Street, to the famous 9th Floor, from
where, in the days of its influence and power, the Communist
Party directed and ruled its apparatus. I was led to the large,
impressive office, where Dennis sat in his lonely lordship,
and when I entered the room, I was told, with a cold nod,
to say whatever I had to say. It took me some ten minutes
to say it. I finished. "Very well. You may go," Dennis said.

I stood there, dumfounded. I had come fifteen thousand
miles. I had seen the last phase of the awful famine in Ben-
gal. I had interviewed men whom no other American had

spoken to. I had seen things of enormous social importance. All this aside from the fact that I was then well known in my field in America, the author of a number of national best sellers, and respected as a writer of some little distinction at least.

Yet none of this interested him. He had no questions to ask me. He had never seen me before, yet even a simple inquiry as to my health was not forthcoming. He merely dismissed me with an impatient wave of his hand, as he would brush dirt aside.

This sounds like a small matter, even an unimportant matter, and indeed there were a hundred other moments of equal shame and worse indignity; but never in all my life have I experienced anything like it outside of the Communist Party. Not even the warden of the Federal prison where I served a sentence as a political prisoner years later ever treated me or anyone else with such inhuman disdain and contempt; indeed, the warden I refer to was a man of heart and compassion; and only in the Communist Party from Communist leadership have I experienced myself and seen directed toward so many others such an attitude toward people.

At this moment of which I write, I went from Dennis to the offices of the *Daily Worker*, on the floor below, and poured out my experience to Joe North, an old friend of mine and someone I loved and trusted. He listened understandingly and then told me how exactly the same thing had happened to him, not with Dennis but with an earlier Party leader, in 1939, when North returned from Spain.

"But why?" I begged him to tell me. "Must men lead

this movement without heart or curiosity or any relationship to people?"

Joe North had no answer except to shrug hopelessly; but others laid such sensitivity as mine at the door of "bourgeois baggage." Many years would still have to pass before we could understand and write about—as I shall further on in this book—the frightful process that produces Communist leadership, that produced a Stalin and a Khrushchev in Russia, an Ulbricht in Germany, a Rákosi in Hungary, a Gheorghiu-Dej in Rumania, and so many more, so very many more.

Many years would have to pass before we would finally know and believe what so many had already known, that the trials of Zinoviev, Bukharin and Trotsky were part and parcel of this dehumanization of so-called leaders into a bureaucracy of terror, murder, and fear—an incredible swindle exercised on decent folk the world over; and it would also be years before we would be personal witness to enough to overcome any and all scruples against leaving this organization.

My learning was hard and slow—too hard and too slow for an explanation of why I remained to have meaning to any but those comrades of mine who also remained. Pride—you would not run away when the movement was under fire; responsibility—whatever these leaders were, they were of your movement and they were in jail and you did not walk out on them; shame—look at the others who left, and hear what your comrades say of them; fear—can I live with myself if I run when the danger is greatest? And so many other reasons, if one must try to explain this—the hope that the Party would change, foreknowledge of the opinion of pro-

Communists everywhere, who would not weigh the factors that went into your decision, or even know those factors— and stubbornness, too, for I hate those who push me around, outside the Party as well as inside of it!

And even when the power to rationalize weakened ever more and more, it was still capable of exercise. Some things stand out with brittle clarity. I remember the time the then Rumanian Ambassador invited half a dozen of us who were on the board of the Communist cultural magazine, *Mainstream,* to have lunch with him. He called for us at our dingy office with a great black diplomatic limousine and drove us in style to the restaurant where we would share an enormous repast. But when we got there and he started to lead us in, his driver remained sitting in the car. We were stupid Americans and unlearned in the higher niceties of Communist practice. Those who were there with me will recall how we quickly whispered together, and then were compelled to ask where the driver would eat.

The Rumanian Ambassador informed us that he, the chauffeur, was a disciplined Communist, and would just sit there until we came out. Feeling that the driver was also a human being, we suggested that he should come into the restaurant and eat with us. After all, we were of a "working class" movement and not yet adept at distinguishing between Communists and human beings. But the Rumanian Ambassador was horrified and aghast at our suggestion. How in heaven's name could we think of sitting a chauffeur at lunch between a diplomat and intellectuals, even if the intellectuals were a little seedy and even if the chauffeur was a Communist?

A little thing—but it bit deep into us, and I remember

how we wrestled with it, trying to down our own anger, for was this man not the trusted ambassador of a socialist nation? But it was sickening—the more sickening years later when I was able to put together the story of anti-Semitism, brute terror, the firing squad and the knotted whip in "socialist" Rumania.

The power of rationalization shrank. Years had passed since that incident with Dennis—and the more I looked back, the more difficult was my own role in terms of my own understanding.

4

Yet I did not leave the Party. Quite to the contrary, I said to myself that I would fight this sort of thing with my own expression of what the Party is and means. "Dennis is not the Party," I said—and then through the years, the list lengthened. "They are not the Party," I said, we said, thousands of rank-and-file members like myself said. I had not entered it lightheartedly or thoughtlessly; nor would I leave it, run away the first time my ego was bruised or hurt. I forced myself to develop contempt for those who were hurt again and again until they left. They were weak, I told myself—we told ourselves.

Almost consciously, I began to acquiesce in a developing situation where other forces would join to prevent me from leaving the Party. I did not state that I was a Communist, but I did not deny it. I spoke where and when I was asked. I signed petitions, hundreds of them. I joined committees.

The more troubled, the more hurt, the more sickened I became by a developing procedure, the more I committed myself. I could not analyze then; I could not understand; I only knew that from the time I entered the Party, I had always teetered on the edge of what I considered to be the breaking of faith in the supreme struggle of men of good will. Therefore, I committed myself. I found myself at Peekskill, leading a fight with my bare hands for my life and the lives of hundreds of others. At one point, I knew I would die in that terrible fight at Peekskill; and I almost welcomed death as the one certainty I could distill from the continuing nightmare.

I went to prison, and after I came out of prison I lived with fear; fear was my companion day and night, fear of the ugly gods who had entered my life, fear of arrest, fear of assault, fear that harm would come to my children, fear of prison, fear that some sick stool pigeon would begin to invent lies about me, fear of frame-up, fear that I would be expelled from the Party—an unfulfilled dream of certain Party leadership—and thereby cast out of the only world left to me.

Again and again, I risked my life—as if I had to prove what I knew to be a cruel lie, that this was worth dying for. I did the things that were asked of me. I gave thousands of dollars, but it was not enough. I wrote a book about what had happened at Peekskill and gave all royalties to the Civil Rights Congress, but when I sold the book at meetings, it was whispered about that I was enriching myself. When I was forced to publish my own books, literally draining myself and my family of all our savings from the years of my success, it was again told that I was enriching myself. I felt I must publish the books of other Communists who were blacklisted, and this again cost me thousands of dollars; and again I meekly accepted the charges of aggrandizement.

Again and again, in financial crisis, this or that part of the Party would come to me for money—and I would in turn go crawling to the rich progressives I knew. I would listen to them curse and slander the Party, even as they curse and slander me now for leaving it; I would bear their insults, their arrogant superiority—so that I might come away with five or ten dollars for the "cause"; and often enough, I would lie to the Party leaders about completing my mission of self-abnegation, taking my last few dollars from my pocket instead.

And yet I did not leave, but clung to the faded, tattered vision of a world of justice and equality.

But neither the process nor I could go on forever. There came a day when I read the words of Nikita Khrushchev—how grateful I should be to him— and then, at long last, I was released. I came awake. The fear stopped, and only disgust and sorrow remained.

I had left the Communist Party, and I had awakened from a long, and terrible nightmare; but months would pass before I could write about the essence of this nightmare—before I would be able to look upon it with some objectivity and say to myself,

"I have only one important task in front of me—to define this thing, to explain it, to picture this unholy god in his own frightful nakedness; so that if there is another generation in my land that must face the agony of my generation, they will never see this avenue as a road to any future that man should face without loathing."

5

As you read these pages, you may well ask where I am going. It has already been asked of me a thousand times; for I think it is a quality of men of good will that they see our brief time on earth as a passage toward some high and meaningful good. Thus the destination becomes of supreme importance. Yet even when the destination has become an article of faith almost akin to a certainty, there are those who see it as secondary to the particular road.

For me, the destination has remained unchanged—the total brotherhood of man, a world-wide entity of love and creativity in which life is neither wasted nor despised.

For many of us, the road that led toward this was through the Communist Party; and for all too many of us, the road became more important than the destination. In time, the road became sacred and real, whereas the destination blurred into increasing unreality.

I hold that some things are sacred, but the Communist Party is not one of those things. I believe that the life of man is sacred, and hardly less sacred are his dreams, aspirations and marvelous achievements. I hold that each forward step of man—toward freedom, justice and equality, away from the darkness of ignorance, superstition and enthrallment —I hold that these are sacred; but there is nothing sacred about the forms he adopts when necessity presses upon him.

In what follows, I shall narrate something of a particular experience of a writer within the Communist Party of the United States and hence as a part of the world Communist movement. This is not a record of disillusionment, for a broadening of knowledge and a deepening of experience must be the very opposite of disenchantment. Nor am I bitter. If I and so many others have paid a considerable price for certain knowledge, it may be pointed out that no knowledge comes cheaply and that others have paid in larger measure.

In what follows there are many things that will evoke anger and resentment from various people—and some of them will hold that these things are better left unsaid. But to me, at this point, the only criterion of what should be said is truth. At least, I will make the attempt to be as truthful as I can.

That statements of mine will be denied I do not doubt. Very often I rely completely on my memory, and memory is a difficult thing at best. But I can say that, to the best of my ability, I have scrupulously avoided any distortion.

I think it also necessary to spell out my reasons for publishing this book; for undoubtedly this question will be raised in many places. From the time I first read the Khrushchev secret speech I have held to a single conclusion, driven home then and confirmed by later events—that the Communist Party in the form we know should cease to exist. I know that this represents, on the world scale, a proposal very far from the reality, even though many forces are beginning to operate to that end. In each of the countries of the earth this question will be dealt with according to the will and the ability of the people of that particular country.

In America, however, a different situation prevailed.

Due to the particular historical experience and memory of the American people, the proposal for the self-liquidation of the Communist Party of the United States was most practical during June of 1956—the month that presented us with the secret speech. Hundreds of influential American Communists came to this conclusion, with pain, heartbreak and great sincerity. Many of them gave public voice to this desire. Others raised and discussed the proposition only in inner Party circles.

This was my own position. I believed that only by honestly stating the situation to the American people and to the world could the Communist Party of the United States retain that thing which we had all treasured so highly for so long, its *honor*. That we in the rank and file of the Party were honorable people I have always held—and still hold. I held that history had made it incumbent upon us to say:

"We had noble dreams and aspirations. We tried as best we knew, and we never betrayed what we accepted as our beliefs and goals. Now, however, because we are indisputably and unchangeably a part of a vast international movement, we must pass new judgment upon ourselves, in terms of new knowledge. And in the light of this new knowledge, presented to us now as irrefutable proof, we have failed. Only one thing can preserve our honor and integrity —to confess our failure boldly and openly; to warn the American people and the people of the world of the awful dangers inherent in our form of organization, and then, finally, to dissolve this organization once and forever. Simple faith in the American people and the American working class should assure us that by so doing we will not weaken the continuing struggle for American democracy and social progress, but rather strengthen it."

Now, in retrospect, I can say that if a Party convention had been held then, in June of 1956, the Party would have been liquidated. By every stratagem and trick at their disposal, the leadership postponed the convention until the inevitable resignation of people of conscience assured them of victory—in the sense of business as usual. In my opinion, the Communist Party of the United States has thus lost whatever claim it had to honor and integrity; and if this small essay convinces those who support it, or even a few of them, that the Party has lost step with history, then it will be worth while. I do not believe that a Communist Party can be destroyed by force. A Communist Party is an idea—and ideas cannot be dealt with in terms of force. It is time we learned this. An idea must be bent over the anvil of truth to see if it can survive some strong blows. I do not believe that this particular idea can so survive.

6

I had the curious experience of witnessing my own extinction and learning how it felt to be and yet not to be—and additionally, never to have been. It came about in this fashion:

On the morning of January 31, 1957, the telephone in my office rang. It was Harry Schwartz of the New York *Times;* he told me that he had just received the current issue of *Fortune Magazine* and had read there that I was no longer a member of the Communist Party of the United States. Was it so? he wanted to know. I said that it was quite true.

That issue of *Fortune* was devoted to the Communist Party and the Soviet Union, and in preparing it reporters from the magazine had interviewed a number of people on the staff of the *Daily Worker,* John Gates and myself among them. In the course of a long talk, one of the *Fortune* reporters asked me whether I was currenly a member of the Communist Party. I answered very definitely that I was not. I had written my last article for the *Daily Worker* in the previous June, and about a month later I had made it plain to certain associates of mine in the Party that I no longer considered myself a member or subject to discipline of any kind.

As a matter of fact, I had ceased to pay dues or engage in any of the regular functions of a Party member more than a year before this. But when the reporter from *Fortune* pressed me for a date, I pointed out that it was impossible to give one and that, unless a public announcement had been made formally, an exact date was meaningless. He agreed to state simply that I was no longer a member of the Party.

I felt that this would be news to no one. Months before, on June 12, 1956, in my last article for the *Daily Worker*, I had written in reference to the "secret" Khrushchev report to the Twentieth Congress of the Soviet Communist Party:

"It [the report] is a strange and awful document, perhaps without parallel in history; and one must face the fact that it itemizes a record of barbarism and paranoiac bloodlust that will be a lasting and shameful memory to civilized man."

The language was plain, and in the rest of the piece my attitude was equally plain. Yet when *Fortune* appeared, I discovered that the public announcement of my leaving the Party was of consequence as news. The *Times* asked me to give them an exclusive interview.

At first I refused, and stated that I had absolutely nothing to say on the subject. I was no longer a member of the Communist Party. That was the long and short and the end of it. Mr. Schwartz' argument was that, regardless of what I felt, the entire press would very soon descend on me, and the newspapers would print what *they* pleased, not what *I* pleased. On the other hand, he stated, the New York *Times* would print the exact text of an interview, no more, no less. I then asked him whether he would agree to my seeing the final copy before it was printed and give me the right to reject it, and this he said he would discuss with the editor. He phoned back half an hour later and said that the editor had agreed.

In this manner I ceased to exist and began never to have been in one-sixth of the earth's surface. I specify this because it has an importance that goes beyond the plain fact of a public announcement. I was quite aware of Harry Schwartz' reputation as an unfriendly specialist on Soviet affairs, and I myself had attacked him bitterly in the past. But since the matter at hand was a public announcement of my separation from the Communist Party in terms of an exclusive interview with the New York *Times,* I cared not a fig whether Mr. Schwartz or anyone else signed his name to the piece, so long as question and answer were printed truthfully. And in this the *Times* was scrupulous.

In this feeling I have not changed an iota; yet the angriest denunciations hurled against me subsequently were not for the contents of the interview but for the fact that Mr. Schwartz conducted it. The anger of certain Soviet writers in particular was directed thus—not against what I had said but against its association with a particular newspaperman. This is not surprising, for in a way it signalizes the whole tragedy of the world Communist movement—a fanatical worship of dogmatized means and an increasing inability to comprehend the ultimate end. Perhaps the best definition of a fanatic is one who, having lost sight of the end, dedicates himself to the means.

Before that time I had been honored by the Soviet Union as were few living writers, Russian or otherwise. Millions of copies of my books had been printed and sold there. One book alone, *The Passion of Sacco and Vanzetti,* had an initial printing of half a million copies. Two of my own plays had been produced there, two other plays had been dramatized from my books, and another book of mine had become the basis for a Soviet opera. Dozens of critical articles had been written about my work, as well as two book-length critical studies that I know of. The Russian critics and the Russian readers were warm, receptive, over-generous and extravagant in their praise. Both praise and affection went far beyond the reality of my work—which is not to say that I was not pleased by it. I know of no writer so objective that extravagant praise beyond the worth of his work is not greeted with pleasure.

In the course of years I had developed a copious correspondence with people all over the earth. My life as a Communist was very open; I have always detested concealment and conspiracy as unbecoming and degrading, and I wrote openly to whom I pleased. Thus I developed a large correspondence with Soviet citizens concerning my work; and never a week went by when I did not receive three, five or a dozen letters from Soviet students, children, teachers, workers, critics, engineers, scientists and so forth, telling me what they had liked or not liked in my writing.

An airmail letter to the United States from the Soviet Union takes between two and three days to arrive. The interview in which I publicly announced my separation from the Communist Party appeared on the morning of February 1, 1957. On February 4, 1957, I received my last mail from the Soviet Union—with the exception of two letters from two officials of the Writers Union, of which I will have something to say later. In other words, a gate had closed; a curtain the very existence of which I had so hotly denied in the past had been quietly drawn. The Soviet post office had quietly and efficiently halted and seized every piece of mail addressed to me; for no one apart from the Party bureaucracy knew that anything was different about Howard Fast. Not one word concerning my interview in the *Times* was published in the Soviet press for seven months, not one word concerning a theoretical statement of my position published a month later in *Mainstream,* an American left-wing periodical.

On February 1, I simply ceased to exist on one-sixth of the earth's surface. All reference in retrospect also ceased, so I not only was not but had never been. A play of mine, *General Washington and the Water Witch,* was currently being performed in the Red Army Theatre in Moscow; the performances continued, but no reference to the play appeared in the press again. The millions of books continued to be read, but the author disappeared from being and memory. Thus, within Russia, no anger, no attack, no argumentation, no refutation, no criticism—but simply a negation. I was not.

Consider this, and you will understand something of what I felt. I had been prepared for anything else—rage, persuasion, mockery, even the possibility that the reaction might be civilized to the extent of stating, "Well, Fast has the right to do as he wishes. We don't judge him by what organization he belongs to but by what he does. He has the right to join the Communist Party or leave it as he desires."

Instead, the question and the answer were both blotted out. Yet it was less important that I ceased to exist in one place than that I had a very real awakening in another. For more than a year now, I have lived with the feeling of a man who has come out of a deep and distorted dream. After long years, I have found myself—my own personal freedom, which I hold the most precious thing man knows; the right to do as my own conscience dictates, correctly or mistakenly; the right to error, blunder and even prime foolishness; and also the right to think, dream, hope and never hold silence when I see wrong and evil done. I know of no substitute for this. Eight months before leaving the Party, I made a public pledge in the *Daily Worker*: that I would never be silent again when I knew of injustice. What follows now is some part of my own experience, which in the end led me to the above statement.

7

There is an addendum to the above, almost in the way of a footnote yet a little more than that. It was a moment of bitter decision, the moment in which I ceased to be a Communist forever; and it turns upon a pledge not to remain silent when I know that I must speak. I will speak to the harm of no man and name no man ever as an individual, if naming him brings him before the face of injustice, him in his own turn. I supply no information in that sense; but when men coast on the awful tides of history, they must be spoken of. The story of this moment of bitter decision is the story of such a man, but I cannot name his name, for it would bring death to him. Therefore I will never name his name, or even the name of the country he represented, and you must take the story on my word.

He will know that the story is true, and others will recognize the genre. I call him the Diplomat.

Elsewhere in this book I have made several references to a column I wrote that was printed in the *Daily Worker* during June of 1956. I publicly left the Communist Party in February of 1957. The column I refer to was a bitter denunciation of the lack of civil rights and liberties in the Soviet Union. Between the appearance of that column and the public announcement of my leaving the Party, a number of diplomats and newspapermen from some of what are referred to here in America as the "satellite nations" sought me out. Some of them were very highly placed persons in the foreign service of their respective countries; others were less highly placed. Because I had written as I had, because of my past reputation, and because I, as a part of the Communist movement, had openly ranged myself against the Stalinist forces in the Communist Party of the United States, they felt free to talk to me.

They talked. They spread before my already tortured eyes such a picture of terror, injustice and sheer nightmare as to make the Khrushchev secret speech appear to be only a moderate outline of a never-to-be-itemized whole. They talked coldly, they talked with passion, they talked with hatred. Some wept as they talked. Some lived over the agony of dear comrades murdered by the Soviet secret police, of men tortured and beaten, of men robbed of every sense of their own human quality. Some cried out, in strangely the same words, "We have learned how to wait. My land will not be another Hungary." Others said, "We will wait and wait. History has a way of being truthful."

But one of them spoke in a calm key—never raised his voice, just spoke to me over a luncheon table in such quiet, simple tones as one uses about the weather. So quiet and simple that there was never room for doubt. He spoke of the pall of fear over his land. He talked about the enshrinement of ignorance, the curse placed upon those who offered either disagreement or fresh opinion. He told about how the Communist leaders who ruled his country lived—their sleek black limousines, their servants, country homes and bejeweled wives, their mistresses and passions. He talked about the crumbs that were left to the people. And, because he was a Jew, he talked about anti-Semitism. And the most dreadful part of it was that he set forth the hatred of Jews as a matter I knew about—both long and well.

When I explained that it was something I knew about neither long nor well, but only recently in the case of Russia and not until that moment in the case of the other nations that called themselves "socialist," he was both astonished and abashed, as perhaps he had reason to be.

In any case, if what he told me was new to me then, it is not new to many people today. Some of it I would like to put down here, but I cannot. And the reason is that when we rose to leave our luncheon table, he said,

"I must do something that makes me deeply ashamed of myself—because my very mention of it impugns you. Yet I must, if not for myself, then for my wife and children. I must tell you, Mr. Fast, that if my delegation should learn, not what I told you, but simply the fact that I met with you alone, I will be arrested when I return to my homeland and in all likelihood will be put to death. I am not pleading for myself; but my wife and children need me. It is hard for a woman and children to be alone today in what my country has become—harder for them than any joy on my part in continuing to live."

Thus this man and myself both came to understand the stuff out of which our dreams were made. I could say, that there, but by the grace of God, went myself; he could not. I could leave the Communist Party and live; he could not. So in that sense he, this nameless Diplomat, becomes the ghost or spirit of this book. It is of his agony, multiplied a hundred thousand times over, that I write; my own is insignificant and unimportant beside it.

8

In America some anti-Communist groups have made a *mystique* of why people join the Communist Party, which in turn leads to an even more puzzling question—why they leave it when they leave it. That this has a peculiar and particular relevance to the intellectual cannot be denied, for the worker leaves the Party quietly through an act of simple withdrawal, whereas the intellectual so often makes an assertion of his departure.

It may be said that Marxism—and the Communist Party, in its claim that it and it alone can carry Marxist theory into practice—appeals to two sections of modern society as a necessity. The worker embraces Marxism in terms of his own intimate struggles and needs as a worker; the intellectual embraces Marxism in his need to find avenues to understand reality and the truth of reality, without which understanding he is frustrated and truncated. Here I am not arguing the validity of Marxism; I am trying to explain it as a force. Businessmen, lawyers, physicians may or may not become Marxists; with them it does not loom as a necessity in terms of their work and life. With students, artists and writers it very often does.

It is not simply the rebellion of youth. That can take many forms—crime, drugs, insane driving in hopped-up cars, senseless defiance of adults, premature drinking and smoking, and so forth and so on. The youth that turns to Marxism, however, engages in a specific rebellion against a society that obscures instead of clarifying, against ignorance, dogma, superstition and apparent senselessness in the relationships of masses of people. The fact that the Communist Party develops and demands a dogma of its own does not alter the facts stated above, nor does it explain why so many restless, alert and inquiring intellects are to be found in its ranks.

Nor are these to be equated, the Communist Party and Marxism. It is quite true that the Party elevates Marxism as its own philosophy, but it also stifles Marxism, corrupts it and degrades it—even as it degrades so many people within its own body and organization.

I came to the left-wing movement out of my own poverty and hunger and despair in the early 1930's, and I came to it out of a working-class background, but I joined the Communist Party in 1943 because I could no longer see any future as a writer unless I was able to wed my principles to action. At that point I did not feel that I was moving away from the traditions that had shaped my thinking, but rather in the direct line of them. Where I had been alone—or at best a partner in a confusion that equaled mine, a frustration as great—I felt that I had now become part of an edifice dedicated singularly and irrevocably to the ending of all war, injustice, hunger and human suffering—and to the goal of the brotherhood of man.

Thirteen years later a man in Moscow closed the doors of a great hall and read to the people assembled there, all of them Communists gathered together for the Twentieth Congress of the Soviet Party, a secret report concerning the actions of the leadership of this party over the past three decades. The report did not long remain secret. It burst upon the world as the most terrifying and incredible account of bestiality, murder and the inhumanity of man to man to appear in our century—and lest this invite comparisons in an era not noted for absence of inhumanity of man to man, let me underline the fact that I refer to the *document itself*, not to a comparison between measures practiced in Russia and these elsewhere. The document, the Khrushchev "secret report," is an itemization prepared by many of the very men who participated in the frightful crimes itemized. In that way, as such a document, it is unique.

With the appearance of this "secret report," the edifice that I had become a part of thirteen years earlier came crumbling down in ashes—ashes of grief, horror and hopelessness.

Since that day a thousand essays have attempted to formulate a theoretical *rationale* for what had happened; and some of these essays, written by sincere and heartbroken men, shed much light on the march of circumstance. Yet I sometimes think that incident can be as revealing as theory. We who in our youth and hope and pride had pledged ourselves, our lives and passions, to justice and brotherhood made no wedding with wickedness. Intimately, I know only the Communist Party of the United States; yet of this tiny organization I can say, honestly and forthrightly and under oath if need be, that never in so small a group have I seen so many pure souls, so many gentle and good people, so many men and women of utter integrity.

And unless you are ready to accept this as the truth, coming from a man who has broken with them and cannot call them comrades again, you will not even begin to understand the most complex and incredible situation of our time—and perhaps of any time in all human history. Nor will you understand what follows here.

9

From the moment of the publication of Khrushchev's secret report, no intelligent and informed Communist doubted its validity. We had known about the report for weeks; we had heard summations of its contents; and there was a fairly trustworthy rumor current as to how the State Department had come by the copy they had—a rumor later confirmed by certain Eastern European diplomats. Apart from that, neither the State Department nor the New York *Times* manufactures material of this sort. To do so would be not only stupid but tragically damaging, for even a simple denial of the origin of the document by the Soviet Foreign Office would have placed both Mr. Dulles and the *Times* in an utterly untenable position.

But they had no fears on that score. They knew, as we in the Party did, that thousands of copies of the report had been printed by the Russians—what accounts for this colossal stupidity on their part, heaven only knows—and were already circulating among the leadership of many Communist parties. They knew that the Russians could not issue a denial, nor did they—until a year later, during his television interview, Mr. Khrushchev mumbled his silly nonsense about "forgeries." And we, in turn, knew within hours that not a word in the report had been tampered with. It was incomplete; some matters were too terrible even for that ghastly record, and these were deleted, not by the State Department but

originally by the Russians; but what was printed in the
Times was an exact translation of the original.

And within twenty-four hours we on the *Daily Worker*
had made our decision to print the full New York *Times*
text in the *Daily Worker*—incidentally, so far as I know, the
only Communist Party paper in the whole world to do so.

This was the result of a set of circumstances into which
I will go somewhat, for they have both bearing and importance in terms of what follows. Later on I propose to
deal with some aspects of Communist leadership within the
Party as differentiated—and it is, most sharply—from the
rank and file of Party members. For the moment I only wish
to note that from the first reports of the Twentieth Congress
of the Soviet Party, early in March of 1956, until the appearance of the Khrushchev secret report in the New York
Times on June 5, there was a virtual abdication of the
national leadership of the Communist Party of the United
States—with the single exception of John Gates who, as
editor of the *Daily Worker* and in conjunction with the
other editors and leading staff members, became for all
actual purposes the national leader of the Party during that
brief period.

Not only was Gates singular in that he was the only
national leader of the C.P.—so far as I know—to be loved,
honored and respected by the rank and file, but he was also
the only one who was bold in spirit, alert in mind, courageous in action and unafraid of the impact of ideas. His
five years in a Federal prison had been years of thought and
study as well as years of mental anguish—and I well remember him saying that after he had read, in prison, that once

forbidden* book, Orwell's *1984,* he had looked at himself and the Party and the Soviet Union with the awful horror of recognition. Yet he could face this, even as he had faced the Fascists in Spain, the Fascists in World War II, and the years of prison to follow.

Within the Party, and particularly on the *Daily Worker,* the reports of the Twentieth Congress had come as an explosive force of mental liberation, not because of their content—the secret speech was still secret—but because there appeared the first trace of iconoclasm in any Party congress in our memory. It was little, but it was enough for us on the *Daily Worker* to seize sledges and begin to break the cursed images with the zest of a drowning man gulping air. Everyone on the staff joined in to one extent or another. Myself, I struck out in every direction with a joy I had not known for years. A whole group of us in the Party had been secret believers in psychiatry, silenced so long by the dreaded threat of expulsion for those who took the name of Freud with grace. Now I could defend Freud and the science of the mind. I was able to lash out and say that the idiotic Soviet doctrine of "cosmopolitanism," where it was not nonsense, was anti-Semitism. I was able to curse capital punishment as a shame to the human race and to socialism in particular. I was able to charge that the Jewish people were prisoners within the Soviet Union. I wrote about my love and ad-

* Like all effective censorship, this is self-imposed. When sufficient contempt and hatred for the author is generated among the membership, a process of name-calling, unthinkable accusation and slander that degrades the undesirable writer to subhuman status, then the rank-and-file member will find that he has no desire even to open the book. The very sight of it is offensive. It must be admitted that this very effective method is not limited to Communist Party practice.

miration for my own native land, the United States, and comrades of twenty and thirty years in the Party came to me with tears in their eyes to thank me and embrace me. I am specific as to my own subjects because I have all the clips before me as I write, but doing much the same thing were Alan Max, Joseph Clark, Ben Levine, Bob Friedman and others. These men on the staff of the *Daily Worker* carried forward an independent editorial stand that set the *Daily Worker* apart from any other Communist paper in the world. It is too often forgotten that of all Communist papers, only the *Daily Worker* under the leadership of John Gates and Alan Max, printed the secret report. The *Daily Worker's* bitter criticism of the subsequent crushing of the Hungarian revolution was equally unique.

And in all this, because they had never coped with thought, ideas, change and the excitement of shattering an idea that was worthless and senile, the national leaders of the Party were quiet. We had the feeling that they had crawled into holes to hide from this tempest that was blowing through the intellectual corridors of the Communist world. We spoke of them with shame and looked upon them with contempt and disgust; like the king in the old Andersen fairy tale, they were so pathetically naked!

But what a time that was for us! What freedom! What glory in the realization that all the years of waiting, mental hiding, intellectual servility, were not for nothing! We said to each other that we had known, that we had been right in not leaving the Party, that the core was good and healthy and bright, and would yet make a marriage with the lovely goddess of reason. We opened the pages of the *Daily Worker* to hundreds and hundreds of letters. We printed everything, the crackpot, the lunatic, the diehard, the sober and thoughtful, the literate and the illiterate, the wise and the foolish; and for the first time in our memory a free, open discussion spread like fire through the Party. Everyone had something to say—except the national leadership. From their mental dugouts, not a shot was fired.

Finally they spoke. Not ideas, not change, but a whining approach to remove John Gates from the paper and expel him from the Party. The staff laughed at them. "If Gates goes, we all go," the staff grinned. So the "leaders" retreated and joined the discussion, saying the same things they had said for years in the same numb, senseless, tired language they had used for years. But their main weapon, the source of all power, had for the moment been blunted—the power to expel from the Communist Party any and all who disagreed with them, who seriously challenged their thinking or their actions; and thus, within the legend that had been erected, to expel that same person from the friendship of those he had spent his life with and from the society and respect of a whole area of men of good will, to turn an independent mind into a "criminal" mind, to do what in Russia was capped with torture and death—to do it short of physical destruction but to leave the human soul seared and broken.

The final bankruptcy of this strange factor in the Communist Party that is euphemistically called "leadership" came on March 28, when the United States Internal Revenue Department committed the last in a long string of repressive measures taken against the Communist Party. Having found a dubious tax case against the Party, federal agents moved into our offices, took over, seized what they called "assets"—a collection of dusty morgue files and ancient office furniture—and by attempting to close down a daily newspaper through such peripheral devices, violated every tradition of a free press in America. There was a bitter irony here, for they chose to do this at the very time of our revolt against the prison of thought we had inhabited for so long.

At that moment Eugene Dennis, then general secretary of the Communist Party, was at home writing a speech. A whole generation of Communist leaders, having put religion behind them, had embraced a newly erected structure of magic. The ritual of this was that miracles could be performed by invoking spells. A resolution was such a spell. A political book was such a spell. A particular speech or statement was such a spell. This use of incantations was divorced from almost every reality of plain people. It did not matter whether anyone attempted to put the resolution into force; it did not matter whether anyone attempted to sell or read the book; it did not matter whether anyone heard the speech or statement. All that mattered was the magic ritual of writing, and from that all things were supposed to flow. For years it was a sorry joke among the membership that few read and fewer could make sense of *Political Affairs,* the theoretical journal of the Party; the important thing was not that it should be changed to make it readable, but that it should exist, thereby performing the act in its silent being.

Upon such a ritual Eugene Dennis was laboring when people were frantically telephoning from the *Daily Worker* to tell him that the Party newspaper had been seized. He was indignant and angry that he had been interrupted in his work. All that day and the following day, we fought and won a fight to save the paper. We wrote it in other offices; the editors put it together, literally on their feet and in motion; John Gates was tireless, defiant, fencing with the Federal men, snarling at them like an angry bulldog; and one grand and brave left-wing lawyer, the Darrow of our time if any man is, fought alongside of us all that day and the next. What a proud time that was! It did not matter whether we were a Communist paper or a vegetarian paper or the New York *Times;* alone, we fought for the finest tradition of our democracy, and we won. They had seized the offices, the assets, the morgue, the typewriters and blue pencils and all the rest; yet we proved that a fighting paper is in the hearts and hands of the people who make it, not in a suite of offices.

And all through that time, with the exception of John Gates, not one national leader of the Party turned up to give us strength, leadership or confidence. The members came; devoted, hard-working, tired, they came with their dollars and five dollars—but the leaders remained away.

Do I dwell too much on this question of leaders? They are not accidents, abortions, sports and misfits who have wormed their way into the organization; they are the terrible logic of such an organization—as I will demonstrate later —even as the gentle, selfless, and endlessly sacrificing men and women who comprise most of the rank and file of the Communist Party are also part of its logic. It is not simple, not to be tossed off with a slogan of either the Left or the Right, not to be put to bed with philosophical patter, not to be dealt with as the government chose to deal with it:

it is to be comprehended, understood and brooded upon, for it is of our time and possibly one of the most important factors of our time.

Leadership and the monolithic party of Lenin! What a tragic moment it was when the Russians, after detailing the most unbelievable horror of modern times, blithely assured the world that it was all due to the "cult of the individual," as they put it, and that now the cult of the individual had been extinguished and all was over. No analysis of what made these individuals into the monsters they were, no analysis of the organization they led, no mention of power and paranoia, no hint that perhaps a "benign" tyranny begets less-than-benign tyrants—no hint of reason. When one embraces magic, why bother with reason? Say "cult of the indidivual," and all will be well.

Yet it was a Russian diplomat who told me that for the last seven years of his life Stalin met with no worker or peasant, only with his own kind, his own lackeys. A Russian diplomat told me of Beria's record as a womanizer—a practice of leadership not unfamiliar to us here. A Communist newspaperman, returned from Russia, held us spellbound for an evening, detailing Khrushchev's record of butchery and quick execution. A foreign minister of another country in the same general area said to my wife and myself one evening, weeping as he spoke of the Russian leader's execution of his own comrades, "We Communists taught the world a lesson in how to die with dignity and courage, but when it came our turn to die at the hands of those murderers, they denied us even the small solace of dignity. They beat and tortured us until we lay at their feet and confessed to the unspeakable crimes that they had invented and written down for us to sign."

Yes, I went to many diplomatic affairs, for my books were then popular in those countries—until the cry of agony made it impossible to go to any more. A diplomat from still another Eastern land said to me, fervently, "We will live with our pain until in its own good time the Socialist Soviet Union will cast out this filth—and then we will cast out our own."

He spoke of leadership—Communist leadership, and he was himself a Communist. That must be understood. To speak of these things and condemn socialism is to be short of sight and shorter of understanding. The lords of the Communist Party are not socialism; they are not Russia; they are not even their own party. They are products of that party. It is a platitude of the worst kind to say that these men built socialism in the Soviet Union—and if any-one thinks so, he should read Khrushchev's secret speech and decide whether Stalin and the collection of hangmen and murderers around him were builders of socialism or terrible enemies of socialism. By the testimony of Khrush-chev himself, it was in spite of Stalin and his lickspittle crew that the Nazis were defeated, in spite of them that a new land arose out of the ashes. Not from enemies of Russia, but from Russian diplomats, I first heard Stalin defined as a man who met doubt, inquiry, independence with one simple sentence, "The truncheon—beat, beat, beat, beat, and then beat again." What a force resides in socialism that it could have the clawing weight of these beasts upon its back, and still build what was built in Russia—for such men as

I speak of build nothing but tombs and create nothing but fear and sorrow. And as they now squirm and twist and develop their palace plots against each other, it becomes more and more evident that somewhere underneath, among the plain people who live and love and work and build, a tide of anger rises that bodes them no good.

10

Let me return to the time I spoke of, the time of freedom of thought and action in the Communist press that began early in March of 1956, full of faith and hope in a rejuvenation of the Party, and then started to fade in June of the same year, the June of the Khrushchev secret report.

The speech was published in the New York *Times* on June 5. The next day the staff of the *Daily Worker* met in Alan Max's office. We had all read the speech. The somber terror of it was in our eyes and on our faces, and now the discussion was whether or not to print it in the *Worker*. In the course of that discussion, something happened that will remain with me until I die. It could only have happened then, at that time, for the truth we saw was brutal, cold and terrible beyond description. Few of us were any longer young. Most of our adult lives had been given to this movement. All of us had made great sacrifices, accepted war and prison and poverty, faced death on one occasion or another. Here were brilliant careers given up, success and wealth bypassed by some, respect and honor abandoned by others, all of us together in a tiny minority group that had been hounded and persecuted for a decade, all of us driven by and wedded to the splendid dream of brotherhood and justice, which even now flickered fitfully, all of us knowing each other so well and so long! And in this group, compelled by an idea and realization that had fastened upon me, I rose in the course of the discussion and said,

"I wonder if there is any comrade here who can say now, out of what we know and have seen, that if our own Party leaders had the power of execution, he or she would be alive today?"

They all looked at me, but no one broke the silence. We had come to the end of a road, and we knew by what grace we were alive. We knew it—and oh, what a terrible knowledge that was. Each one according to his talent and ability—some better, some worse—had given his life to the cause of mankind, the brotherhood of man—and we knew that for this the reward was death.

That may appear at first glance to be a merely "dramatic" statement, but it is sober truth. All sorts of explanations have been forthcoming for the record of execution and torture itemized in the secret report—which is, incidentally, only a part of the whole frightful story. Perhaps the most ridiculous is the Russian one, the notion that a "cult of the individual" can explain what happened—and it is typical of the shoddy thinking among Russian leadership today. Others, among them highly placed Russians, talk of Stalin's "sickness" and "paranoia," a curious development in that nation which so violently interdicted modern psychiatry. Unquestionably, Stalin was sick and insane, but was this limited to Stalin? The killings itemized in the report are not threaded together by any line of reason, purpose or plan; but neither can they be ascribed simply to the lunatic blood lust of one or two men.

The fact of the matter is that all the victims are marked

with unorthodoxy of one kind or another—sometimes overt resistance, sometimes only a word or two, seemingly innocent, but enough to bring death from Stalin. Sometimes the unorthodoxy is embodied in a false accusation, an anonymous letter, a rumor, a whisper—but always the accusation.

We who were gathered together at the *Daily Worker* staff meeting had unorthodoxy in common. We knew it. The leadership knew it. Some of us were bitterly hated and resented by the leadership; I know of no one present at this meeting who was more than tolerated. The knowledge that had come to us as a culmination of all our experience was not a realization that the leadership of the Party was paranoiac or bloodthirsty, but that the pattern of death as the final outcome of iconoclasm was a built-in part of the C.P. structure. Why paranoiacs exercise this power of death is another matter, which I discuss elsewhere in this essay. And however this statement of mine may be denied today, it held at that one moment of clear and frightening knowledge.

So the terrible, terrible secret speech became a reality for us—not because of what had happened in Russia, but because of our experience here in the Communist Party of the United States.

11

Since writing the above, I have gone out of my way to ask at least a hundred well-informed people whether they had read the text of the secret speech. This group included a number of ex-Communists as well as several people who prided themselves on the completeness of their curren information. Only one of the entire group answered that he had read a substantial part of the document, and even he had not completed it.

All through this essay, I refer to this speech as the pivot of my thinking, the single factor that more than any other was to determine my action. I readily admit that a good many of the facts presented in the secret speech were given a public airing by anti-Communists at one time or another during the past twenty years; but I also think that any objective observer must admit the very great difference between accusation and proof. By me, as one who believed fervently in the justice of the Soviet method, circumstantial evidence was rejected in the face of Soviet denial. Proof became operative for me when this great body of "slander" was collated into the declaration of the nominal leader of the Communist Party of the Soviet Union.

But this same proof was not operative for the people who did not read and study the Khrushchev report—and I know of no way in which this can be remedied. There is

53

no question in my mind that the secret report had vast "illegal" circulation in Hungary before the revolution there took place, and I am equally convinced that it acted as a catalyst for that revolution.

This same catalytic action could be observed in the Communist Party of the United States upon the appearance of the secret document, and I have described some of the effects. In a sense, many more pieces of the puzzle than the report alone contained were thrust into place. I make mention elsewhere of the facts reported by the Polish-Yiddish Communist Party paper *Folkshtimme,* which opened the hideous Pandora's box of anti-Semitic murder. Presented with the unbelievable list of great Jewish writers murdered by the Russian secret police, we had a basis for working out much of the puzzle of what had been—for us who believed in Russia—an utterly unbelievable state of affairs. Belief and disbelief always exist within a framework.

Soon after this revelation—I think in July of 1956—a Party member came to me with the proposal that we frame a document as an open letter to the Soviet leadership, demanding some explanation of the anti-Semitic atrocities in Russia (still unexplained at this writing, I may observe).

I framed this document, to be signed by prominent American Communists, and it was presented at a special meeting called for the purpose. John Gates was there, the only one of the Party leadership, and Morris Schappes, the Jewish historian, also attended. In the course of the discussion, Schappes told of a series of articles in the Manchester *Guardian* by a British reporter who covered the trial of a number—twenty, I believe—of elderly Jews in Moscow. These Jews were accused of the possession of "Zionist" literature, and for this fiendish crime they were sentenced to three to ten years each.

As Schappes spoke, he noticed the growing expression of horror on the face of Gates, himself recently released from prison, and then Gates asked, "Under what law?"

Schappes mentioned the particular article in the Soviet criminal code, and added, "A law, Johnny, ten times worse than the Smith Act."

Now the fact that neither Gates nor I nor a number of other people in attendance that night knew about this law —under which a Soviet citizen can be sent to prison for ten years for having a copy of the New York *Times* or any similar material in his possession—spoke poorly for our information; but more important, we believed the account. In other words, the basis for belief had changed; our entire understanding of Party procedure had shifted; and our point of view was at that moment radically different from what it had been before. And though the people present lacked the courage to expose themselves as to the document, they did in the course of the evening give vent to their horror and disgust.

I reject in no uncertain terms the glib explanation that the type of procedure expressed in the secret speech can under any circumstances be considered as revolutionary necessity. Any student of the Russian revolution knows that during its initial years it operated as a mighty liberating factor; the type of repression described above became operative in the 1930's. Today, for the first time since Stalin and Stalinism took power in the camp of socialism, it is possible to put a whole picture together out of evidence offered by Soviet and allied spokesmen. At this moment the weight of evidence is massive, all too massive for me to even begin to itemize here; but even the introduction to that body of evidence compiled by Mr. Khrushchev is utterly convincing, if people will only take the trouble to read it.

I suggest reading it, not to further slander or sully the Soviet system, but to make it possible for the world to move forward toward peace and social justice. So long as Soviet socialism as led and practiced by the Communist Party can claim a monopoly of progress, then no clean winds of freedom will blow over this earth. And the fact that colonial peoples struggling for their freedom are backed by communism and turn toward communism proves nothing—except that Russia is a good deal cleverer than we are in the present power struggle.

I speak now of a man who went to the Soviet Union about a year ago. He went on behalf of the Jewish Commission of the Communist Party, and he took with him many questions to be answered. He was a loyal Communist then and he remains so—although this passes my understanding.

When he returned, he sat in my office for two hours and spoke to me. What he said as a trusted American Communist and what I listened to could not have passed between us a year before. The possibility for saying and listening was provided by the Khrushchev report; it bound us to belief and understanding, and because of this he was able to narrate an unspeakable and frightful history. Finally, quoting a Pole, a man highly placed in government and Party councils, sober and trusted, he said to me,

"Howard, you must understand that this is no small matter, no peripheral matter, but central to everything. [The Pole] told me in all seriousness that, in the course of this murderous business over the years, some fifteen million people felt the direct effect of the terror in prison and concentration camp—and some five million of them died."

I refused to believe, and I said so, and he answered with great sadness and surrender,

"I also refuse to believe it. I cannot believe it. Only—I know it is true."

If Communists doubt the above story, it will be easy enough for them to find out what man I refer to; and I ask them to ask him whether I lie or not. He will remember clearly enough, although he never spoke publicly in such terms.

To forget this—and move on? Business as usual? Remain silent and the infamous report will be forgotten? But can one possibly do that and remain a man?

The secret report is central. For years Trotsky was the devil's own name, and no Communist was permitted to read him, much less quote him. But a few weeks before writing this, I opened Leon Trotsky's book, *The Revolution Betrayed*. I had not looked at it for almost twenty years, but its words rang with the terrible timeliness of a commentary on the Khrushchev report written today. Yet the book was published in 1937.

I care little at this point about denunciations by Communists, but I feel impelled to suggest that the right to challenge me be earned. I defy Communists to read the secret report again, fully, carefully, and then to balance against it Trotsky's *Revolution Betrayed*—and having done so, to refute me. As for those who will not read the evidence, their minds are locked and the Party has had its way with them.

12

In what has already been written here I have tossed out a few pieces of a very complex puzzle. Like a scattered jigsaw, they bring up more questions than answers; yet they are only a few, a very few, parts of the whole. In an effort to simplify an amazing and subtle process—and the writer, always within the limitations of a given number of words and pages, must either simplify or wallow in confusion—I have made certain arbitrary separations; and if it now appears that the Communist Party is composed of leaders who are devils and a rank and file of saints, I am at fault. That is certainly not the case. There are good, honest decent folk among the leaders of the Party, and among the rank and file there is a very substantial section of crackpots, bigots, fanatics, automatons and fools.

I was trying to indicate that the dynamic organizational force and structure of the Party tend toward two very different poles—a power-hungry, dictatorial, inhuman and anti-human direction in the leadership, and a confining, thought-constricting, submissive and frustrating direction among the rank and file. Both of these tendencies arise from the structure, practice, lore, and body of symbolic magic that is the Communist Party; and since these are tendencies in an organization of human beings, there are a great many exceptions to the rule.

This I propose to show in what detail I can. I do not

know that anyone can realistically understand the Commu nist Party without a long experience within it, but certainly one can come closer to the truth of it than is demonstrated in the legends of either the Left or the Right.

The central and basic intent of this book is to do as the title suggests, to relate the effects of a union between the writer and the commissar. In its entire history, the Communist Party is threaded through with the experience, allegiance, love, hatred, exaltation and agony of writers; and by virtue of this very situation, the public's knowledge of the Communist Party tends to be a reflection of the writer's relationship to it. While there is a certain deep validity to this, it is only a part of the story. As far as I am concerned, what happens to the writer within the Party is meaningless unless the Party itself is understood to some extent.

The Communist Party is a monolithic structure, dedicated to unity of purpose and exaltation of leadership; whereby it is understandable that two of the most abhorred internal tendencies are *antileadership* and *factionalism*. Even if the Party is torn asunder within, it turns a monolithic face to the world and denies that factionalism exists. All through the period of the "Gates Faction," a term constantly repeated in the newspapers, the Party leadership denied that any such split as that between the "Gates Faction" and the "Foster Faction" existed.

Yet it did exist; and the very fact that the Gates Faction was antithetical to the classic form and nature of the Party made the defeat of that group inevitable. The supporters of John Gates were a widely assorted group, and their thinking covered a broad range. Essentially, the group stemmed from the original revolt of the *Daily Worker* staff under the leadership of Gates himself. During the period of a few weeks between the government's seizure of the *Daily Worker* and the appearance of the Khrushchev secret report, the Gates Faction seemed to be in the ascendancy; but my own belief is that the Gates Faction never represented a majority of the Party, and that their initial success rested only upon their moral position as contrasted with the utter bankruptcy of their opponents. Many of us then believed that if we moved quickly and decisively, we could seize control of the entire Party, find new leadership of decent, honest and humane people, form a democratic, humanistic movement for socialism—and perhaps light a spark that would fire the imagination of the entire world Communist movement.

It is true that numerically the Communist Party of the United States was insignificant; but it was the Communist Party of the most powerful nation on earth, and therefore it had an importance far beyond its size or effectiveness. If this dream had become reality, perhaps interesting things would have happened; but in retrospect it does not seem possible that it ever could have become the reality. In the Gates group were people who wanted to reform the Party, others who wished simply a change of leadership, others who desired to do away with the practice of "democratic centralism," still others who wished to change both the name and basic structure of the Party. In addition to these, there were a substantial number who felt that the only and ultimate logic of the situation was to liquidate the Party, stating honestly and publicly why they believed it had failed and why it must not persist in our country as the political form through which to achieve socialism.

I myself was one of this last grouping; and I am convinced that the most important reason for the defeat of the Gates Faction was that, reduced to its basic logic, it could call for only liquidation.

Many other reasons have been given for its defeat. Some spoke with awe of the dirty and unprincipled tactical infighting of the Foster Faction, old and experienced hands at this sort of thing. Others spoke of the fact that hundreds of the best and most independent minds in the Gates Faction quietly left the Party before the Gates group was fought to a standstill and defeated at the national convention of the Party. So long as the Foster group stood on the grounds of preserving the Party essentially as it was, the rebels were doomed to defeat. Nor was this simply because the others in the Party, the people who did not support Gates, believed in the senseless intransigence of the Party leadership.

We at the *Daily Worker* staff meeting I described earlier were not the only ones who saw the wedding of an organizational pattern to torture, brutality and death. Many others in the Party understood it just as well. A few weeks after the secret report was published, an old friend of mine from Detroit came to New York and spent some time with me. Through all the years I had known him, I had always regarded him as the finest type of American worker, a huge, burly Irishman, born in Detroit, who had a part in all the struggles of the Detroit workers to build the great auto union. For the past several years he had been persecuted, harried, blacklisted from every factory in the area—because he was known as a left-winger. He said to me,

"Howard, no matter where I went, no matter what they said to me, no matter how they cursed me out, they always knew that I had no price tag on me. They hated me, but because I was a part of dignity and honor, they respected me. Now I have no dignity and no honor. Where do I go from here?"

In the end he remained with the Party, not because he understood less well than I the horror of what the Party had produced, but because the Party had given him as a worker the only hope and sustenance he ever had known. Let the middle-class man live with his illusions of the American worker as another middle-class man in a slightly lower income bracket than he himself! The facts are quite different. The worker may have refrigerator, washing machine and auto, but all hang on the thread of time payments, and to meet those payments he works like a degraded machine. The inside of a steel mill is not the inside of an air-conditioned office, and the comfortable chair I sit in as I write this is not the equivalent of an assembly line. The worker lives trapped in a rut that degrades him mentally and breaks him physically, here and in Russia too. And if the great majority of the American working class ignored the Communist Party, it nevertheless offered to the handful who joined it at least the right to dream of and hope for a time when the dignity and reward of a man who worked with his hands would be at least the equivalent of the rewards offered to so many who do no work at all in the real sense.

For many intellectuals there remained a possibility for hope and dreams, a voice, other organizations to join, other directions; but for the worker in the Party—well, who else would offer him a dream of hope and equality, not pie in the sky but something rooted in the reality of his shop and his bench? With the Party in existence, he could hope that it would change; but with the Party liquidated, what would take its place?

Thus he argued and moved—and that too contributed to the defeat of the Gates Faction. Indeed, it sometimes seemed that the closer and more intimate one was with the actual organizational functioning of the Party, the better one understood the awful logic of the secret report, the more surely one could confirm it and understand it in terms of one's own experience. I think it was also the case that many of those who had made the greatest sacrifices for the Party saw more clearly than others what its functioning nature was. I myself know at least twenty paid functionaries of the Party, men and women who have devoted their entire adult lives to it, who have left it—bitter, too deeply wounded ever to function within it again, and too conscious of its inner workings to believe ever again that this could be the instrument for the liberation of mankind.

On the other hand, I remember well the reactions of a sweet and cultured lady my wife and I have known for almost twenty years. A woman of intelligence, talent and public position, married to a world-renowned scholar, she telephoned the day after the publication of the secret speech to express her hope that I had not wasted my time reading it. I replied that I had read it twice, most carefully, and asked whether she had.

"I do not," she replied, "read State Department forgeries or anti-Soviet slanders. In any case, nothing could change my attitude toward the Soviet Union or the Communist Party. I know them both too well."

But she had never been to the Soviet Union, and her

knowledge of the Communist Party, of which she was not a member, stemmed only from a social relationship with some of its members, fine people whose courage and constancy she adored. Nothing could shake her, and to this day nothing has. As with her, so with her husband, and so with many others whose relationship to the Party was based on similar grounds.

In the same vein, it should be noted that not all people read a thing just because it is published. And when the published document consists of more than twenty-five thousand words of small type, is framed in less-than-engaging English and monotonous and dreary in its long record of horror, brutality and murder, very few people indeed read it. Yet it still amazes me to meet so many Communists who have glanced at this document in only the most cursory fashion, and so many others who have not read it at all—and particularly is this true of the Foster Faction. All sorts of reasons are given by them—doubt as to its validity, time, misplacing of the text; but none of these are meaningful. It would be more truthful for them to say that they are afraid to read it, as many are; others who began it put it down out of sheer inability to face the accumulation of horror; and still others, through long years of trying to read the strange language and hazy reasoning of Communist leaders, have built permanent barriers between themselves and such documents.

It should also be noted that a certain kind of non-Party sympathizer was unequivocally hostile to the Gates point of view. Among these was a body of very wealthy upper-middle-class people, many of whom I knew. Their total relationship to the radical movement consisted of grudging gifts of money —money that had to be pleaded for, begged for, to the humiliation and degradation of those who asked for the money, not for themselves but for the cause they believed in. The FBI has expressed the opinion publicly that these people were sons of struggle and went into battle with their hearts and purse strings open; but the FBI was woefully wrong. These people walked no picket lines; they were not seen in the mass struggles of the past decade; they did not work endless hours without reward or remuneration; they gave only money, and precious little of that. Yet when the intra-Party rebellion took place, they were the first to call us renegades, stool pigeons, opportunists and FBI agents. In the apartment of a millionaire *rentière*—who will not speak to me now, for she considers me a renegade—I heard the wealthy owner of a chain of restaurants, a former saloon-keeper not fit to wipe John Gates' feet, call Gates a "traitor, opportunist and renegade." A millionaire factoring banker referred to Joseph Clark of the *Daily Worker*, screaming as he did so, as a "lousy agent of the FBI." Another woman slipped off her five-thousand-dollar mink coat as she said, "It has to be one way, the only way. You're going to have civil war, barricades, and the workers are going to have to fight and die until blood runs like water in the streets!" She panted with appetite as the workers' blood ran like water; and I thought to myself then, "What awful guilts do these people have that they think they can wash away with their crazy dreams of barricades and rivers of blood?" Never had I heard a Communist talk in such terms; but these sick people, who had seen no other death than a painted corpse in a funeral parlor, no other violence than an auto crash —these people literally lusted for an Armageddon their mad dreams had promised them. A businessman at this same gathering, whose doll-like wife carried a price tag of ten thousand dollars in gown and jewels on the hoof as she stood, raged at me, "So what if twenty-five thousand people died in Hungary! You got to pay a price for this kind of thing."

For what kind of thing? For the rape of Hungary in the holy name of the Bolshevik Party? For the piping echo of the words of the atom-maniacs who would offer the blood of half a nation on the altar of their insanity?

"Yellow," he cried. "You, Gates, Max—the whole crew of you, yellow—yellow!"

I would hesitate to write this scene into a novel, for it has no sane justification except its truth. This was a handful in one room; but all over the nation the mental revolutionaries, the parlor pinks, the living-room warriors, the mink-coated allies of the working class wept that people like myself had betrayed the holy cause of communism.

As one of them said to me, "Fast, you've stepped over the point of no return."

But at least I know what I stepped away from. You pay for knowledge, and I have picked up some of it here and there. There is always a price to pay, and I don't complain of the price I paid for my knowledge of the Party. My soul is not bruised, nor am I disillusioned; those are not the results of knowledge. I think I came to understand something. Perhaps I am wrong, for I have been wrong enough times to make a barrel of it. On the other hand my conclusions might be worth listening to, for they come out of a good deal of reflection and experience.

13

All too many Americans have come to think of the Communist Party and the Soviet Union and socialism as various names for the same thing, and many such people are astonished to learn that even in the Soviet Union, where Party membership brings privilege and power, there are only about eight and a half million Communists. On the other hand, many Party members of long standing equate the Communist Party and socialism, holding that the latter must remain a chimera without the former, while still others state that there can be no socialism that differs importantly from Soviet socialism.

It is not my intention here to discuss socialism, either practically or theoretically, although I feel obliged to say that, while I firmly believe that all peoples of this earth will find their way to socialism in their own way, no socialism thus created will be Soviet socialism or particularly like it. My point at the moment is the Communist Party.

This party cannot be equated with socialism. Socialist theory derives from the dreams and hopes of centuries—dreams and hopes that were finally subjected to scientific analysis and underwent historical-materialist development at the hands and through the minds of Marx and Engels. The Communist Party, as we know it in most of the world today, derives from the particular Russian experience of Lenin and other leaders of the Russian revolutionary movement, stem-

67

ming initially from the events of the end of the nineteenth century and the beginning of the twentieth century. Many books and many millions of words have been written concerning the struggles and factions within the Russian social democratic movement during the period when its majority faction (*Bolshevik*—the Russian word for majority) fought for and finally gained control of the movement; and while these documents are of great interest and importance, it is not within the compass of this short book to summarize this aspect of Russian history or even to quote copiously from the many documents.

As a matter of fact, unless one has the time and energy and background for a very long and detailed study of that period, any attempt to set it forth in brief will only compound confusion; for the host of documents of this period, including some of the work of Lenin, have now taken on, to some extent, the shape and substance of a body of mystical-theological dogma, and have been used in a fanciful and metaphysical manner by a whole generation of Communist teachers. Thus, through an equating of two historical periods half a century apart, and two social situations entirely unrelated and unlike each other, Communists have used this body of dogma not only as a point of departure from the present reality, but as a means of proving through "scripture" whatever conclusion they have reached previously.

Thereby a mirror was held up to show where the Communist Party came from, while the questions of what it actually was and where it was going were almost entirely ignored. My intention here is to say something about the Party itself, particularly as I have come to understand its operational course through long association and specific observation.

In that curious and strangely written book, *History of the Communist Party of the Soviet Union,* which has been a textbook for a whole generation of Communists all over the world, there are surprisingly few clear references to the tactical thinking that went into the creation of the Communist Party of the Soviet Union. The subject of the book frequently has the ghostlike attributes of a new god, and even more often the holy authenticiy of a deity, but its own shape remains a mystery. Nowhere in the book is there a clear and precise description of how the Party actually functions, although it is referred to, possibly over a hundred times, as a "new type" of party. Unfortunately, the few pages of precise information that would make clear to a reader how this "new type" of party differs specifically from an old type of party are missing; and though we are treated to bizarre and often incomprehensible accounts of how the Bolshevik Party's organizational and theoretical purity was successfully defended against counterrevolutionary attacks by "Trotsky-ites," "Zinoviev-Kamenevites," "Bukharin-Rykovites" and other groups, we are never quite sure of what the core of the difference actually was. We are told in detail what the Bolshevik position was on dozens of questions, but we are never informed of the details of how this position was arrived at or what other minority positions were—except in cases where the minority position was public property, its supporters for the most part safely executed and interred.

In all, it is a most curious book, written in a language all its own, filled with venom, gutter adjectives, and simple declarative sentences apparently worked up out of a thousand-word primer of "basic English." Yet it is the major text of the Party that the world knows. Originally, we in the Party were told that the book was a collective work, compiled by a college of the leading "Marxist" thinkers in the Soviet Union—which statement was also used to explain its lack of grace, style or any literary character whatsoever; the point being that it contained wisdom, not rhetoric, grammar or style.

We were also informed that the fourth chapter of the book—an almost vulgarized simplification of dialectical materialism—was particularly to be noted, since it came from the hand of the master himself, none other than Stalin.

It is to be understood that when, from 1946 on, all reference to the book from the Soviet Union named Stalin as its sole author, we were naturally confused—the more so since the book lauds Stalin in the third person from beginning to end. Whereupon we were told that Stalin did not actually write the book but merely inspired it, and that the authorship designation was more or less against his will and in tribute to the esteem in which he was held. Then, when detailed accounts from Russia spelled out his "act of writing," we were told by our harried leadership that they were as amazed as we were, and that the important thing was the book and not who wrote it. Finally, an answer to this interesting problem appeared in the secret report as follows:

> . . . As is known, *The Short Course of the History of the All-Union Communist Party (Bolsheviks)* was written by a commission of the party Central Committee. This book, parenthetically, was also permeated

with the cult of the individual and was written by a designated group of authors. This fact was reflected in the following formulation on the proof copy of the *Short Biography* of Stalin: "A commission of the Central Committee, All-Union Communist Party [Bolsheviks], under the direction of Comrade Stalin and with his most active personal participation, has prepared a *Short Course of the History of the All-Union Communist Party (Bolsheviks)."*

But even this phrase did not satisfy Stalin: The following sentence replaced it in the final version of the *Short Biography:* "In 1938 appeared the book, *History of the All-Union Communist Party (Bolsheviks), Short Course,* written by Comrade Stalin and approved by a commission of the Central Committee, All-Union Communist Party (Bolsheviks)." Can one add anything more? [Animation in the hall.]

As you see, a surprising metamorphosis changed the work created by a group into a book written by Stalin. It is not necessary to state how and why this metamorphosis took place.

I dwell on this only because this is the "history" of the Party—and because this history is mainly responsible for the notion that the Communist Party (in its organizational form and theory) sprang full blown from the mind of Lenin, even as Athena sprang from the brow of Zeus. Its familiar explanatory name became "the Leninist type of party," a very handy title, since it gave Stalin and the men around him the authority of a priesthood guarding a holy altar. Although in the *History of the Communist Party of the Soviet Union,* constant reference is made to Lenin's works for the "fundamental and decisive part" they played in creating the concept and form of the "new party," the only categorical explanation of the "new party" in the "history"—vague though it is—is framed in the words of Stalin, if indeed he was the author. I quote it below, from page 142 of the American edition:

> After the expulsion of the Mensheviks and the constitution by the Bolsheviks of an independent party, the Bolshevik Party became firmer and stronger. *The Party strengthens itself by purging its ranks of opportunist elements* [italics in the original]—that is one of the maxims of the Bolshevik Party, which is a party of a new type fundamentally different from the Social Democratic parties of the Second International. Although the parties of the Second International called themselves Marxist parties, in reality they tolerated foes of Marxism, avowed opportunists, in their ranks and allowed them to corrupt and ruin the Second International. The Bolsheviks, on the contrary, waged a relentless struggle against the opportunists, purged the proletarian party of the filth of opportunism and succeeded in creating a party of a new type, A Leninist Party, the party which later achieved the dictatorship of the proletariat.

It is this passage, not the words of Lenin, that defines the Communist Party in the "history." I believe that this book—authored by Stalin or otherwise—was put together sometime in 1938. The American edition, published by International Publishers, was issued in 1939. The act followed the series of purges which are described in the book as the "liquidation of the remnants of the Bukharin-Trotsky gang of spies, wreckers and traitors to the country," and the so-called "history" was itemized by men still wet with the river of blood that flowed from the executions, still enchanted with the melody of pain under torture. It is evidence after the fact, and the definition does not describe what the Party was intended to be by Lenin or anyone else, but what it became in the hands of Stalin and his circle of executioners.

It is quite true that Lenin, in his thoughts concerning a new revolutionary party for Russia, insisted "that such an organization [the new party] must consist chiefly of people *professionally* engaged in revolutionary activity" [the italics are mine], but there is no evidence that he ever intended this party to become the programmatic tool of its "professionals," and it is most unlikely that he ever dreamed that there was coming into being a self-functioning instrument for creating and perpetuating a bureaucratic hierarchy of these "professionals."

In fact, certain Communists, some with long experience in Russia, some of great age and knowledge, have lately assured me that Lenin, in his last days, was filled with horror and fear by the developing nature of the Party, but this can only be taken as their own findings in the rumor mill. If Lenin wrote of these specific feelings on his part, such writings have been destroyed—and certainly no statement to such effect has come officially from the Soviet Union, nor should it be expected in the near future.

At this point, let me attempt to describe the organizational structure and operation of the Communist Party as I have known it in the United States.

A picture of the Communist Party can best be gained by examining it from its base to its apex, for it is essentially a pyramidal and monolithic structure. Within its framework, this structure is capable of a good deal of variation and flexibility, but whatever the variation from country to country and from period to period, the operational framework remains essentially the same. Here the picture is of the Communist Party of the United States in the decade after World War II, but I am sure that it will be recognizable in other places.

The base upon which the Party structure rests is its *branches*. There is a practice among professional anti-Communists of calling them "cells" and "units," but these are merely shock names and are absolutely nondescriptive. In American terms, the branches should be described as "clubs," for that is precisely what they are. They are the equivalent of the American political club. They can vary in size, depending upon the circumstances, from five to over a hundred members. They are the rank and file of the Party, the functioning mass base of the Party, and rarely if ever are their premises disturbed by the presence of top leadership. They can be formed in neighborhoods, shops or communities, or among professions. They are the political home, the club, the functioning base of the Party rank and file. They almost always contain a majority of sincere, scrupulously honest and dedicated people. They also almost always contain a minority of nuts, crackpots and frustrated souls—but this is the case with most similar organizations in America.

These clubs are concerned with the interests and problems of their immediate area, and frequently their work is good and constructive. They are guided by the needs of the people they know, and most often they fight tirelessly for the fulfillment of these needs. They face endless difficulties and very often are totally unable to surmount them. They are not "professional revolutionaries" for there is practically never a paid Party functionary on their level, that is, within the clubs. Their work is volunteer work in the purest sense, and many of them work tirelessly and with intense dedication, even with a continuing and frequently shining sense of the sanctity and nobility of the cause to which they are wedded.

Unless the above is understood, there is no use in even discussing the Communist Party. It is precisely because so many look at the Communist Party from the premise of initial evil and malevolence that it remains, to the non-Communist world, the greatest mystery of our time. But millions of decent people do not voluntarily join an organization of evil premise. They do not fight and sacrifice and die for it. No one considers himself a purer patriot than the Communist rank-and-filer, and most often his actions tend to underline this.

And it is precisely because of this intense dedication that the rank-and-file Communist is willing to submit to something that distinguishes his party from all others, an ironclad discipline, perhaps stronger than any discipline the world has ever known before, and a monolithic and vertical pillar of mass thought and agreement. It is the very purity of inception that makes this discipline possible. The rank-and-file Communist judges his organization by his subjective development; his own incorruptibility in a frequently corrupt society makes him so define his organization; his own sacrifice is intensified in his long-distance view of his leaders; his own original intelligence, frequently so sharp and penetrating,

7 5

induces a picture of the Party leadership as composed of virtual gods of wisdom. (It does not pay to quibble over the word "intelligence." When people accept a series of premises, it is not their intelligence that is affected by lack of validity in the premises, but their ability to extend their intelligence rationally. It is the exercise of reason and investigation that is blocked.) The persecution and slander of the non-Communist world, as measured against his integrity and honesty, finally leads him to that most cursed and destructive retreat of crusaders, righteousness; and as righteousness increases, his original method of logic and reason gives way to religious fervor. The Communist Party becomes the Temple of God. If he was ever an atheist, the Communist is not one now; he has renounced and rejected the old gods, but he accepts the priesthood of the new god, and discipline becomes operative.

Discipline in the Communist Party is voluntary, but in the silent background is the sword of excommunication. Without the power and religiosity of expulsion, the Communist Party could not exist as it is. Before the moment of the Khrushchev secret speech, expulsion from the Communist Party was akin to eternal damnation, the body alive but the soul already dead for eternity; and so powerful had this conviction of the membership become, and so widely and sincerely had they promulgated it, that millions of non-Communists considered anyone who bore the label of expulsion from the Party as a lost and damned soul, a corrupt and dangerous human being who no longer owned the right of admission to the society of men of good will. Perhaps no religion in all history had ever exercised such a power of damnation over its communicants; and perhaps no communicants in all history had accepted so totally the theory of a hellish curse of excommunication.

To a sincere and devoted Communist, expulsion was almost as bad as death—and sometimes worse. It is almost impossible to convey to many people what the total implication of expulsion meant. For almost a generation, several million Americans of good will accepted the fact that a man was expelled from the Communist Party either for being a police spy or for utter venality and degeneration of character. Such an expelled person became outcast, not only among Party members but among a circle of progressives a dozen times larger than the Party itself. This was a concept deliberately nurtured and put forward by every Communist Party on earth; for it was basic to Party discipline. Without this ritual of expulsion and its accompanying mythology, the Communist Party would be something else indeed. The expelled Communist thus became the leper-heretic of today, living on under an interdiction unique since medieval times. Needless to say, a very great many of those expelled were guiltless of anything more culpable than the effects of reason or independent thought. So we begin to see the bottom process whereby the vertical pillar of thought and agreement operated.

Before going on, however, I feel the need to emphasize this question of expulsion; for even though it is dealt with in other parts of this book, it remains the most mysterious part of Communist procedure.

This is not in reference to the Russian practice, where expulsion is so often coupled with torture and death—by Khrushchev's own testimony—but to its nonviolent function in the non-Communist world. Nor is expulsion to be equated with a process like excommunication from the Catholic Church; for if the Church deprives a man of salvation, it does not exclude him from the company of good men in this world. Communist expulsion does. While all things are permissible in a non-Communist, the ex-Communist who was expelled is cursed apart from any subsequent action. Even H. L. Mencken, that wise and caustic man, told me of the repugnance he could not help feeling for ex-Communists— so much was he influenced by the pervading curse of the Party on those it dispensed with.

Diego Rivera, to my way of thinking the most fulfilled of Mexican painters, lived under a cloud of sorrow in terms of his expulsion from the Party. He could not give enough to the Communists, do enough—yet it was to no avail. He knew perfectly well that his original expulsion was a matter of personal vindictiveness, yet even his giant stature among the people of his own land could not do away with the pall of expulsion.

A little better is separation of one's own volition, but even the massive evidence out of Russia and the satellite nations during this past year and a half cannot quite overcome the question of separation from the Party. A great many serious and experienced Party members understand precisely why I did what I did, but those further from the Party yet in sympathy with it judge me by the prevailing rules I spoke of.

For example, I received a letter from two valued old friends of mine who are not and never have been Party members. Their knowledge of the Communist Party and its internal operation is hearsay knowledge at best; yet they could see my action in such simple and incredible terms as these:

> If you, Howard Fast, are not satisfied with the techniques of collectivization, planning and coordination thus far developed in the Soviet Union or in some other area where socialist construction is being attempted, you face three possibilities: (1) to join the ranks of counterrevolution and do your bit to slow down its slide into oblivion; (2) to do your part in assisting some other effort to build a collective social apparatus in China, India or Yugoslavia; or (3) if neither of these possibilities appeals to you, to dedicate the remaining years of your life to working out a better alternative than any thus far proposed. . . . We recognize that as a creative artist you are strongly influenced by the desire to create unrestricted and untrammelled. This is a personal matter, and for you a very important one. But for us, for mankind, there are larger issues. . . .

Even granting that there are larger issues than individual freedom, protection against a berserk murder apparatus, and the right to choose one's own form of government—denied to the Hungarians by naked force—my own statements have been directed only against the Communist Party apparatus. Yet such is its pervading power that millions of men of good will the world over equate the Party with every form and hope of social progress. In a world divided sharply and neatly into two camps, reaction and progress, with the Party standing forth as the sole leader of progress, all criticism is stifled. At the same time, he who leaves the Party is cast not only into the other camp, as the Party would have it, but to the bosom of the worst reactionaries of that "other camp."

Unless this is seen as the ultimate of psychological power, the reader will be unable to comprehend the whole meaning of Communist discipline. Never before in human history did an organization allocate to itself credit for every single act that might help to bring mankind a step forward. Never before did an organization possess such enormous powers of destruction and castigation, to be exercised upon any individual who challenged it out of knowledge. It has, in the thinking of millions, utterly equated itself with man's hope for the future; and if one should say that this is a future without grace or morality, one is thereby that most cursed of all things—a counterrevolutionary.

Such is the method of discipline at the base of the Party.

From the broad base of the branches to the apex of the pyramid, the structure develops in this manner. A number of branches are taken to constitute a *section*. There is no predetermined size for the section, and most often it is a matter of organizational convenience. A large neighborhood may define a section, an industry may do so, a trade, a profession—and on this section level, we have the first appearance of the "professional" or paid revolutionary. Yet while it is colorful, it is also misleading to call him a revolutionary; for even if he was so once constituted, he soon becomes a practicing bureaucrat.

The leader of the section is the *section organizer*, who is a full-time, paid functionary of the Party except in times of deepest poverty—and even then some stipend will be found. If the section is small and poor, it has only this one paid functionary. If it is large and can command an adequate income from its members—who invariably give more than they can afford—it also boasts an *organizational secretary,* full-time and paid; and in a good many cases there is a third paid functionary, the *educational director.* These, one or two or three as the case may be, are the connecting steps up the pyramid. They guide the section, and though they work and meet with a section committee from the branches, their major disciplinary function is to see that the line from above rides down to the base of the elevator shaft. At this they have extraordinary skill. They conduct constant and tireless internal propaganda: classes, lectures, intimate talks with members, special meetings, literature distribution and also a process of "clarification"—an interpretation of current events and of the Party line akin to the interpretation of scripture.

This is the lowest and most active—vis à vis the rank and file—level of leadership in the Party, and most often it is the only leadership the members ever come to know. Many of these functionaries are as honest and dedicated as the members. They exist on tiny wages, they have none of the privileges of the apex of the pyramid, and they are in constant contact with the membership at least, if not with the non-Communist world. But others almost immediately become power bureaucrats, planting a seed that will mature later. The awful force that must affect all of them lies in the fact that once they are functionaries, their entire lives, destinies, futures lie in the ascending vertical structure. Unless they are content to go nowhere—a rare state of mind—they can only go up the elevator shaft, and soon enough they learn what are the qualifications for this ascent.

Above them are no rank and file, but only a full-time, paid bureaucracy. Now there are only two directions and two functioning operations: decisions move downward, reports move upward. During this time of which I write, in large industrial states where the Party had sizable membership, such as New York, Pennsylvania or Illinois, the sections were linked into *regions,* with much the same organizational leadership—except that it might include more posts, *trade-union director, literature director,* etc. The over-all management was vested in the *district,* consisting of sections and regions, and most often a district was one of the forty-eight states. The district leadership assumed an importance commensurate with the size and strength of their organization. In certain important districts large offices and staffs were maintained, newspapers and pamphlets were printed, bookstores were operated and a whole host of related operations were undertaken. I need hardly mention that this is not the case today with the present tiny Communist Party.

Above the districts, we approach the apex of the pyramid, the *national leadership* of the Party and the *national office* or bureaucratic apparatus. This apex rules through the districts and downward, supposedly through a large *national committee,* which would ideally include not only functionaries on district and national levels but representative leaders from the trade-union and cultural areas of society. However, in practice, it was limited to paid functionaries; and even these, via the national committee, were not the top of the pyramid. The national committee chose from among itself the actual leadership, the *national secretary* and the *secretariat* which conducted the day-to-day business of the Party.

But as in Russia, so in many other lands and here too; the national secretary became the dictator, lord and ruler of the whole structure.

14

In theory, the Communist Party is democratic, and it has been called the most democratic form of organization ever devised. It is also admittedly *central,* whereby its functioning process is rather bitterly known as *democratic centralism.* Supposedly, it elects its national leadership at national conventions of delegates from every level, but never to my knowledge, except at the last national convention, where the Gates Faction engaged in a struggle with the acting leadership, has a leadership been elected that was not designated in advance by the secretariat and the national secretary. In the Browder case, other forces outside of it were operative; left alone, it can depend on its internal religiosity, its priestly mode of operation and its exercise of discipline to assure the election of those chosen by the apex. Theoretically, the sections and districts can also change or elect their leadship, but in actual operation these areas elect or change only at the suggestion of or with the approval of the apex. I know specifically of half a dozen instances where the national leadership chose district secretaries before the leadership of the district was even consulted.

The national Party apparatus functions through commissions and itself appoints the commission heads. Dozens of paid bureaucrats, some of great power, some of lesser, work in various parts of the apex structure; they are all appointed by the top, and they hold their jobs and authority and prestige by virtue of the top and by virtue of undeviating obedience to the decisions of the top. The general secretary also has the power to remove any district leader he wishes to remove, and, of course, any section leader. This is an operative power contrary to the constitution of the Party, and while it may be fiercely denied by the present leadership, anyone who has had experience with the actual working of the Party has seen it exercised again and again.

Theoretically, the Party line on major questions is determined by a general discussion of the membership, whose conclusions rise to the top and actually determine the line. This is used to justify the claim of intra-Party democracy. In practice, however, the final position is *always* predetermined by the top before the discussion even starts. Sometimes this decision is the result of a meeting of the national committee; sometimes the secretariat determines it; and very often indeed it is a personal decision of the general secretary himself, whose power cannot be overestimated. He makes his decision in the form of a resolution and gives it to the national committee for discussion and they in turn emerge from their discussion with a resolution that is for all important purposes identical. There are probably historic exceptions to this, but in my own experience it has *always* happened thus. Then the resolution descends to the membership for their consideration, while a chosen few, mostly functionaries, expand a *controlled* discussion in the Party press—whose editors, prior to Gates, were totally subservient to the whim, will or petulance of the general secretary.

The membership discussion itself is guided by the paid section functionaries, whose major task then is to beat down and destroy any opposition to the resolution—even if steps toward expulsion must be taken; and while the discussion may continue for weeks, it is all sound and fury. The result, finally, is *always* in the precise line of the original resolution, with only enough formal variations for the membership to reject the notion that they have been made fools of.

What keeps this incredible situation from shattering the whole structure to bits is first and foremost the religious-mystical terror of expulsion with its attendent taboos; secondly, the adroitness of the Party functionaries in convincing the rank and file of the godlike wisdom and goodness of the top leadership; and finally, the faith of the rank-and-file member in the temple of virtue that the Party has become to him. Of course it is to be remembered that in those countries where the Communist Party holds power, torture and death form the final framework for discipline.

In a bourgeois party of the "old type" such tactics do occur; but, lacking both the discipline and the theological development, such parties always split when the contradiction between the aims of the membership and leadership becomes too sharp, which forces a practice of concession and democracy as an inner and continuing dynamic. The Falange, the Fascists and the Nazis also created parties of a new type with their own peculiar disciplines; and while there is no comparison between these and the Communist Party that will hold water, they do make for sober thought.

Some readers will leap to deny this, and will base their case on what the secret report revealed. But whereas the Nazi Party was in concert with the tone of the society it ruled, the Communist Party, wherever socialism exists as an economic system, faces an enormous contradiction between itself and the socialist society it feeds upon. This contradiction cannot endure, but must resolve itself; whereupon the major forces directed against the Communist Party will in very short order —historically speaking—oppose it with a force and determination it cannot survive. The very economics and dynamics of socialist production demand generations of educated men and women—scientists, professionals, artists, people whose very mode of existence demands that they face reality and inquire as to the nature of that reality. A part of the reality they must face is the Communist Party, and they will face it in the large as humanists who cherish life and hate the practice of fear, superstition and ignorance that is Party dogma today.

As a final process, the Communist Party demands from its basic branches, as well as from its middle-top commissions, unanimous conclusions to discussions, as a demonstration of inner Party unity; in which last process the temporary façade of democracy is contemptuously discarded for a totalitarian product.

Thus we have been able to trace two major currents or forces that operate inwardly through the Communist Party. The membership, self-sacrificing, dedicated, and motivated originally by a vision of socialism, justice and human brotherhood, are forced by both intra-Party and outer-world pressures toward self-righteousness, narrowness, religiosity and Party worship. Through this process they transform themselves into a priesthood, the Party into a temple and the Party leadership into gods. These are not merely picturesque symbols I have chosen; they define the fact. I have been through the process, and I know.

The leadership, on the other hand, develop in a different direction. They are petty gods to those below them, but they function as priests to those above them. If they are people of conscience, tenderness and integrity, as they often are, they will never be able to make the hotly contested climb toward power above; for the crown is not to the bold, the inventive, the imaginative or the humane. Quite to the contrary; the test is dogma, the criterion orthodoxy, and the way through unbending rigidity. The requirements include a good nose for the wind, skill at tactical infighting, patience enough to wait out and side with the winner in any inner dispute, a thick skin, a divorcement from the deep needs of people and an unbending devotion to what is called "the Party line." The great danger along the way is to be *wrong,* and since right and wrong refer only to the line of the Party, the tactic is to avoid clear-cut decisions and always occupy neutral ground where you can shift sides at the drop of a hat.

One cannot leave this without mentioning the case of Earl Browder. I have come to the conclusion that, except in cases of personal rivalry, leaders of the Communist Party are removed only when their continuing existence in office threatens the edifice of the Party. Anyone who desires to examine the history of the intra-Party struggles in the Soviet Union—a long and weary task—will see that in every case the existence of the Party structure in its Stalinist form was at stake. When the high priest threatens the temple, he is slain. The logic of Browder's thinking was the liquidation of the Party, and so great was his intra-Party power that he was able to carry through the first steps toward smashing the whole organization—for whatever would have been its final shape, it would not have been ever again a party of the "new type." The Duclos letter gave the rival leadership the support for what they already desired, the elimination of Earl

87

Browder and the restoration of the temple and the priesthood.

It should also be noted that during the recent intra-Party struggle here, about which I wrote, a brilliant defense of Browderism by a rank-and-file member of the Party was the most convincing document to emerge from the discussion. The incumbent leadership spared no effort to suppress and destroy this document.

Before leaving this, it is both worthwhile and interesting to put together a composite of the *Party leader*, for he is the inevitable product of the Party, in any land where the Party is a Stalinist structure—and it is he who dirties the page of history and blackens all the colors of man's dreams. I have seen many hundreds of him in many lands. I have watched him operate in a hundred different situations, among workers, housewives, intellectuals, professionals, farmers and youth. I have seen him in a broad variety of situations—and I have observed him with some care, as you might imagine.

He is not a very impressive man, for you are given to understand that in the Party men are not judged by bourgeois standards. He has a cold and aloof quality; none of the warm handshake and open heart. He is a careful man; he chews his words before he lets them out. On occasion, usually as the result of a considered decision, he will smile a bit and go out of his way to say a few words of chit-chat to a *special* personality; but he is uneasy in this kind of social intercourse.

When asked his opinion on any subject, providing the question comes from an important source, he assumes an attitude and, talking not to you but through and beyond you, declaims the proper one of some few dozen opinions he is always officially provided with. When this opinion deals with anything but the Party line, it is an equivocation. Within the Party line, it is dogma couched in the priestly gobble-dygook that is his substitute for the normal language of his native land.

At a meeting, he is careful to be the last speaker—unless there is present a leader higher in the ladder of command. In that case, he will bow to authority and be the next to last speaker; although, if he is on the power-make, he will use every trick to jockey for finish position. Since fully three-quarters of his life is passed sitting at meetings, the tactic of final position assumes very considerable importance. There are two reasons for this: firstly, it gives the leader an oppor-tunity to assert his importance and aloofness, for the very act of listening so long presupposes certainty; secondly, it allows him to weigh the relative strength and position of the contenders in any argument, to carefully gauge which is the side most likely to succeed, and then to join them with the knockout blow toward weakness. He is out to establish a score for "correctness"; this is the accepted goal, for after all, wasn't Stalin always correct?

His carefulness is exhibited whenever he speaks or writes. He eschews original opinions as the devil himself; he restricts himself to areas of proven safety, where Marx or, and preferably, Lenin can be quoted to back up his position. At infighting, he watches the people on his side build an attack, and then he uses all the points presented to devastate. He always builds bridges, for he is not one to go it alone.

"As Comrade So-and-so pointed out," he is fond of beginning —for Comrade So-and-so will remember and return the favor when needed.

His high moment comes when he feels it is safe to be "sharp" with an opponent; and then he lives. Such a moment comes when his opponent in a discussion or policy meeting is either witless enough or honest enough to persist against the majority. The leader does not "become" sharp unless he is absolutely certain that his opponent is sunk, outclassed and isolated; for there is a certain danger in being "sharp" and many a Party leader tumbled in the running because he tried "sharpness" before a situation for it had developed. Usually, the leader will wait until one or two others on his side have prepared the ground with degrees of "sharpness," after which he wades in for the kill. Now no holds are barred. and the man of ice and reserve allows passion to take over. He is withering in his scorn, contemptuous in his sarcasm, and terrifying in his condemnation. In a land where he is the power, he reads a prelude to prison or death, literally swelling with righteous wrath and purity; in a capitalist country, he is limited to moral destruction—and as he conceives the needs of this objective, he proceeds to humiliate his opponent, or unseat him, or make him an outcast, or require penitence and a plea for forgiveness, or lay the groundwork for expulsion.

All of this builds toward omniscience—for it is toward the cultivation of a mantle of omniscience that his life is directed. The necessary narrowness of his mental process limits him; his equipment is a smattering of ignorance; he is never an intellectual, and any real wisdom would make him throw up his hands in disgust at his own words. His dogma of Marxism cannot substitute for orignal thought and mental reaction—yet omniscient wisdom is required equipment for his role and his climb to the top.

To this end, he learns a bag of tricks which he uses with tiresome regularity. When he must listen to a discussion totally beyond him and on which he can have no safe opinion —and this is often the case—he puffs his pipe knowingly and never says a word. When the chairman of the meeting inquires deferentially whether the leader would not like to make a contribution or sum up, he shakes his head tolerantly. This conveys the impression that, in his wisdom, he has decided that it will benefit the others to work this out for themselves. It also establishes his reputation as a democratic fellow who does not impose his opinions at all times.

Another tactic is to note that the hour is late—and to say that he will present his views at the next session. This not only gives him a few days to sound out the situation, but also establishes his reputation as a man of calm and patience.

Still another method is to listen like a hawk until he can fix one phrase or statement that represents a possible deviation. When he has latched onto this, he throws it in as something so heinous that it overshadows all ideas. He now becomes the single-minded defender of the purity of the Party line. There is no better reputation to build in leadership than a dedicated defense of the Party line.

In matters of art and profession, he faces the greatest difficulty, for he is without taste, standards of judgment, background or any of that sensitivity so necessary to literary or artistic criticism. But here too, he has a few safe and hoary tricks. For one thing—there is always a Russian specialist like Zhdanov, providing he can follow such involved reasoning

—but even without this prop, he manages to operate. By careful listening—together with a knowledge of the relative virtues of the contending groups as to Party line—he can decide which contender has the necessary narrowness and sterility; and then, certain of where "correctness" lies, he proceeds to "associate himself" as the phrase goes, with the "thinking" of this group. He will also manage to give the impression that their thinking originates with him, although he will by no means take any open credit for this.

The drive toward omniscience, which runs like a thread through every action of his life, begins to develop within him a conviction of omniscience; his total mental process is now so structured as to make it impossible for him to face the fact that he is wrong. He operates within the bitter Party remark, "Well, comrade, let's self-criticize you." He knows that Marxism is the "indispensable key to all questions."

He is just sufficiently above man. When favors are done for him, or kindnesses expressed toward him, he does not thank the donor. This is bourgeois. He is the Party; the act of giving and taking is part of the political "reality." Also, he has over the past years lost all power to indulge normal human sentiment; his "carefulness," his "correctness," his fear of slipping in the ascent, the mistrust which lines the road to power—all these combine to cripple his ability to be at ease in the presence of other human beings.

He has no friends. Long ago, he convinced himself that equalitarianism and "democratic centralism" are incompatible. To admit of friends would be to admit of equality, and thereby the magic-autocratic nature of his position would be impaired. There are other reasons which make friendship impossible. Friendship requires small talk—and small talk is a luxury the leader can no longer permit himself. He has eschewed it for too long—in the knowledge that uninhibited talk is dangerous. He only talks "politically." In the Party it is said of the leader, in terms of the highest praise, "He thinks politically." This means that any and every incident of life is fitted into the gobbledygook of the dogma, the cant and the scripture. It also means that the leader cancels out his own impressions and reactions as a human being.

He is never "subjective"; for to be subjective, which means that one reacts to one's personal hurt or pride or need or emotion, is a cardinal sin in the Party. So important and so completely keyed to Party structure is the process of the denegation and subjugation of the individual, as typified in the case of Comrade Kedrov, that the leader must perforce endure the same process himself, so that even though he comes to ultimate power, he has reduced his individual human quotient to the barest minimum.

The leader is married, but only a handful of the rank and file have ever seen or met the drab, colorless, tired woman who is his wife. When he appears at social functions of the Party, or when he is invited to an outside social function—diplomatic or otherwise—as a representative of the Party, he almost always comes alone. This is "political" function, and he does not involve his wife in this. On the rare occasions when his wife is present, she is mute. She may say, "Thank you," or nod, but she does not venture any opinions of any kind. It is taken for granted that she is not "politically" on a level with her husband. Apparently no one in the Party knows whether he has children or what they are like; the subject is tactfully avoided.

There is only one area in the entire Communist mythology where the leader will permit himself deviations and the exercise of humor—and it is understood by the Party that this particular operation of the independent mind is "safe"; that is in the area of what is known, so often euphemistically, as the "woman question." Here theory and practice remain comfortably apart, and the sly quip is both used and appreciated. The leader finds it convenient to establish his reputation for a sense of humor in this area. He makes it plain that however much he may be the cold and stern apostle of the future in all other matters, when it comes to women, he is just a plain, solid, down-to-earth old-fashioned citizen who's ready to get right in there and toss the ball for the old team.

I cannot resist recalling the arrival of the Soviet delegation of intellectuals for the Cultural and Scientific Conference for World Peace that was held at the Waldorf in 1949. When the sincere and tireless young women who had worked so hard and creatively at organizing the entire structure of the Conference saw that not a single woman was in the Soviet delegation, they exploded with indignation and went directly to Alexander Fadeyev, the Russian writer, who was the political head of his delegation. In no uncertain terms, they demanded an explanation of such procedure on the part of a socialist state—which theoretically was dedicated to a solution of the "woman question."

"But we have solved the woman question," Fadeyev answered blandly. "So you see, for us it no longer presents a problem."

This same combination of stupidity, contempt and arrogance marked the answer to every question of propriety of socialist action that we put to the Russians through the years that I was a Party member. In this case, Fadeyev acted in the true sense of a Party leader, combining light humor and contempt. It should also be noted that when, during the progress of the Writer's Panel of the Conference, he was asked directly by Mary McCarthy and some of her friends to explain what had happened to a number of Soviet writers, whom they carefully named, he not only gave his solemn word as a Soviet citizen that all of the named writers were alive and well, but he brilliantly ticked off the titles and description of the work that each particular writer was engaged upon. He told where they lived, when he had seen them, and even repeated details of their merry reaction to the "capitalist slander" that they were being persecuted. So smooth and ready was his rejoinder, so rich was the substance of his quickly supplied background, that one might well credit him with more creative imagination than he had ever shown in his own books. As chairman of the panel, I was quite naturally provoked that Miss McCarthy and her friends should so embarrass this fine and distinguished guest. His conviction and meticulous sincerity were above suspicion, and I think, if I remember correctly, that not only myself but Miss McCarthy and her friends were at least in some measure convinced that he spoke the truth. Like myself, how could they possibly have believed that a man would create such a monstrous and detailed lie and expect it to hold water?

Yet that is precisely what it was, as I learned, through the testimony of Polish and Russian Communist sources eight years later; and all of the men Fadeyev had spoken of so casually and lightly and intimately were, at the time he spoke, either dead from the torture chambers of the secret police or by firing squads, or lying in prison, being tortured and beaten, even as Comrade Kedrov was—to die later.

Still, Fadeyev was less than the typical Party leader, even though he was the "boss" of all Soviet writers and a member of the Central Committee of the Soviet Party. Degraded, his conscience and soul warped all out of shape, hammered into such a hellish image by the movement that once dedicated itself to the salvation of mankind, he remained a writer, a creator—still knit by threads to the agony and passion of mankind. This the Party could not undo, and after listening to Khrushchev's secret speech at the Twentieth Congress, Fadeyev looked into the same dark and monstrous mirror that confronted all of us who still maintained a connection with mankind. What he saw must have been terrible indeed, for he went home, opened a bottle, and remained drunk for twelve days. Then he took his revolver and shot himself through the head.

So he died, and may God, or whatever justice or judgment there is, have mercy on his soul. He was no leader but only a poor wretch driven into a place he could not occupy and live. (The true leaders did not shoot themselves; their shell of righteousness had no weak spots.)

Such, briefly, is a description of a Party leader in the very top echelons of the movement. He is not a pleasant person, and I have often imagined him to be a lonely person. In countries where the Communist Party is in power, he shares fat material rewards. In a sense, the entire country and all its productivity belongs to him, and he has but to lift a finger to have his every want satisfied. But in capitalist and colonial countries, that is hardly the case. Utopia is still over the horizon, and he must satisfy himself with the absoluteness of a state within a state, which every Communist Party is. Since only the psychological forces of discipline are operative, he must live modestly and not extend his privileges out of all proportion to the lot of the membership.

If his party is a small and poor party, he will be proportionately modest in the patterns of his behavior; if the party is large and powerful, he will extend himself and adopt many of the conveniences of living that are at the disposal of leaders in Communist states. But no matter how small his particular party, he has the "spiritual" rewards of a head of state whose rule is absolute. He is final judge and final appeal. He can make absolute decisions and he can command servile obedience. He can gorge his ego. Yet to this end, one other factor is necessary.

Given all this, he must also be driven by a lust for power; for there are few other rewards for Party leadership. The pay is poor, the privileges petty, the dangers great and the struggle long. But the reward of power is enormous; and since power is the drug, the spur and the goal, it is no accident that his own comrades described Stalin as paranoiac. Given a situation where godhood and leadership tend to coincide, where power is the ultimate reward as well as the food of the journey, the paranoiac almost always wins out. It is his particular sick hunger that is allayed, his particular awful lust that is fired and fed and his particular organization of personality that is satisfied with the ultimate place. Let some call such men great; the world has paid an enormous price for their "greatness."

15

People have asked me why I waited so long to leave the Communist Party. Did I know nothing of what was going on? Yet in their questions, they make it all too simple. I joined because I accepted a premise, as so many others did, that only through this party could peace, socialism and the brotherhood of man come to this earth. Certain aspects of history appeared to bear this out. To join the Communist Party is a very serious action; and serious people do not leap in and out of such organizations.

I could not have written what I wrote above a month or a year after I joined the Party. I am, perhaps, not easily convinced; I am also not easily unconvinced. It took years of fact, incident and experience—a good deal of which I will detail later—to come to these conclusions. And above all, it required the catalyst of the Khrushchev secret speech. Only with his contribution, out of the heart of the first and largest Communist Party on earth, did all the bits of the puzzle fall into place. Even then, through my heartsickness, horror and anger, the question of whether this was the result of evil individuals or the historic-organizational pattern of the Party remained. It took months of thought, reading and discussion to make up my mind finally. And it took more months of doubt before I was able to write at any length about this. I know that no analysis of just this kind has ever been written before, and I can sense that it may be of very great consequence. I am writing about people whom I loved as well as about people whom I despised. I am writing about the bravest men and women I have ever known, as well as about petty bureaucrats, mental and physical cowards and power-drugged paranoiacs.

During my time in the Party I had a reputation as an undependable and uncontrollable element. I am not ashamed of that reputation, for it meant only that I clung to my mind and my reason. Charges for expulsion were brought against me twelve times; and each time I fought, licked or evaded these charges. I was determined that I would not be expelled from the Party—at first because I believed in it, later because while I no longer believed, I was determined not to be cast out with the curse of the small creatures who feared me and wished to be rid of me.

I left in my own good time because I had come to the above conclusions. I am neither disillusioned nor depressed, and I have lived through grim times, but times when mankind made gigantic strides forward. Though the Communist Party is disciplined and often splendid in military action, I do not think it can claim credit for the events we have seen. Socialism, justice and the brotherhood of man are mighty and irresistible forces; they will grow to fruition in spite of the Communist Party—and Soviet socialism will not forever lie supine under the heel of the commissar.

Here in America the term "commissar" is translated as "functionary" and as "chairman." But I think it is one of those words best descriptive in its coloration, and among the rank and file of American Party members it is used constantly as an epithet of contempt toward Party leaders they despise. Therefore no other word is precisely right. The commissar, here as in Russia, is in common usage the spy, the watchdog, the petty priest who reports to the high priest, the mouth of dogma and cant, the reader of ritual, the inquisitor, the finger of suspicion and the ultimate witness for execution.

The Communist Party, with its dogma, its religious, pseudo-Marxist cant, its hatred of ideas and invention, creation and change—its priesthood, temple, and fumbling, small-minded gods—is not a product of civilization and sunlight, nor will it last long in a world that can win and keep peace. Its own membership, who have left it in the thousands and hundreds of thousands throughout the world, are coming to understand it. No more can those of us who speak in these terms be dismissed as "Trotskyites" or "agents" of the capitalists. We are going to speak and be heard—and raise a loud voice against any organization that bids men to deaden their minds.

16

The references to magic *throughout this work are made most seriously, and for that reason, I feel, they must be expanded upon. Magic, as used here, is an anthropological designation, and in no sense refers to the type of stage trickery that defines its modern meaning.*

In anthropological study, magic is the name given to primitive science in the pre-religious era of man's development. At this stage of man's progress, magic serves the same function as science does today—being essentially a means used by primitive man to control or temper natural elements, beasts and other men. I do not discuss the effectiveness of magic, merely its purpose; and thereby desire to establish the method as not supernatural but materialist. At that time, the mystical and religious elements in magic were insignificant; it was essentially a process of materialism.

As civilization developed and the evolution of religious thought went on, magic was often associated with aspects of religion; but apart from that phase of magic's own evolution, an appreciable body of magic practice survived in terms of its original purpose, as a science that operated independently of the scientific method and therefor independently of the laws of cause and effect and proof.

Students of magic divide it into four classes, and each of these four classes is integrated into Communist Party thought and practice. So deep and so thorough is this inte-

gration that not only Party members but a whole school of non-Party historical observers have accepted the legitimate use of these processes. Since Marxism is basically a materialist philosophy, its corruption accepts a degraded materialist method. Here is how this method is operative in each of the major subdivisions of magical practice:

1. Sympathetic magic: *This type of magic rests on the proposition that a desired result may be brought to pass by mimicking the said result. It also includes the manufacture and use of spells, and the continued effect upon each other of objects once in contact, though these objects may subsequently be far apart.*

In the Party, *demonstrations are undertaken frequently, and often with tragic uselessness, in the belief that vast parallel movements will thereby be put into motion. The facts of experience have no effect upon this practice. Resolutions are used as spells. Again and again, I have seen resolutions passed with the deep and absolute conviction that they would affect motion; but the repeated absence of any possibility of motion makes the resolutions, in effect, magical spells. Similarly discussions; similarly decisions, thousands of which are made with no thought of ever putting them into effect. Again, this is not cynicism but the total belief in sympathetic magic. Pamphlets are also used as spells. Millions of Party pamphlets have been destroyed in bundles, lie in warehouses or in basements; the acts of distribution and reading have become secondary to the production—the* spell *itself. Involved in this is the fervent belief of Party leadership in the power of their words to change history, whether in verbal or printed form. There are many other examples of this type of magic. There is also the feeling that anyone once touched with Party doc-*

trine will feel the continuing effect of that Party doctrine, regardless of his separation from the source.

2. Divination: *This area of magical practice deals with the obtaining of hidden or secret knowledge. In formal magic, necromancy, astrology, augury, divination from the entrails of birds, clairvoyance and similar methods were used.*

In the Party *and in Party language, this was known as "the indispensable tool of Marxism," which uncovered areas of knowledge otherwise closed. This particular art of divination was not only used again and again to reveal the pattern of the future—as witness the endless economic and political predictions of Party leadership—but also, and so much more destructively, as an excuse for a Party leader to declare himself an expert on any subject under the sun.*

I wish to state emphatically that I am not dealing with parallel methods here, but with the actual use of magic; not with ignorance pure and simple, but with the knowledge of the magician. For example, some years ago, a discussion of aesthetics took place in the pages of the New Masses. *Those of us engaged in the discussion—which had, incidentally, originated in France—were people who had for years, as writers, attempted to study and comprehend the use of aesthetics in literature. Nevertheless we were not competent to decide the discussion. For that purpose William Z. Foster entered the discussionn and put it to rest. Though he was a labor leader and not a creative writer or artist, his grasp of divination assured us that his answer would be correct. (So it was in Russia, where Stalin or one of his bully boys knew all on all subjects.) Another example is the senseless crusade against psychiatry. A former* Daily Worker *editorial writer undertook to demolish the whole structure of mental science,*

*not with study, knowledge and evidence, but with the "given"
power of divination. This same practice of divination, ap-
plied to trade-union and political work, resulted in an almost
endless series of disasters for the Party, yet the method was
not changed.*

3. Thaumaturgy: *Which is wonder-working, the creation of nonreligious miracles through alchemy, jugglery,
legerdemain and the intercession of jinns or demons.*

In the Party, *the practice was garbed in high-sounding
trappings of what we pleased to call "dialectical materialism."
(This is not to be taken as a criticism of dialectical materialism but of a specific practice thus misnamed.) The key word
to the miracle was "qualitative change." It presupposed an
area of wonder-practice that became operative after one had
labored sufficiently at nonproductive and often senseless tasks.
If one did a thing again and again, through the years, one
would reach a point of transition to the desired miracle.*

4. Incantation: *The use and chant of magic formulas.
The use and delivery of magic power words. The magic use
of the names of gods or power beings. The use of magic
ritual procedure. This usage of magic historically bridges
the gap to primitive religion, and many elements of its
formalistic ritual practice survive in the higher religions. It
is not to be wondered that this area of magical practice
should be most cherished by the Party.*

In the Party, *the use of magic formulas and power words
was daily practice; in fact, as the dynamic struggle of the
Party—as during the Spanish War and the 1930's—lessened,
the influence of magic increased throughout its entire vocabu-
lary. Phrases like "Wall Street" and "imperialism" remained
attached in part to reality, but other words such as "Bolshe-*

vik" and phrases such as "higher level" and "bourgeois baggage" and "thinking politically" and "party consciousness,"
etc., have an existence virtually independent of concrete
meaning.

Interestingly, during the free-wheeling discussion period
I refer to in the body of this essay, a Party member with a
sense of humor and an unshackled mind composed and had
published an article consisting entirely of such magic phrases.
Gobbledygook, it read much as the average statement of
Party leadership would read. Communists who have both a
sense of their own language and an affection for it have long
bewailed the mammoth string of wooden clichés used to
preach Party dogma. Not only are these constructions alien
to the normal people's usage of English, but they are also
frequently offensive to the ear. While all of them can easily
be rephrased, they are fostered out of the laziness and pervading sense of magic that underlie Party ritual. The pages
of Party publications are filled with the word "hence," an
outmoded form almost never used in modern speech or writing. When I asked V. J. Jerome for an explanation, he gave
me to understand that it had become hallowed by tradition
into a meaning beyond that of the words "therefore" or "con-
sequently." Take this from "whence" it comes, which is all
I can do.

The use of power words and of the names of power
beings goes along with the above. "Marxism" is entirely
ritualistic as a power word, and such names as "Lenin,"
"Stalin," "Duclos," etc., have the force of incantation. Definitions such as that used for socialism, "From each according
to his abilities, to each according to his work," are not ex-
amined, for then their hollowness would emerge. Instead,

they take on the force of religious-magical chant. Readings from Marx, Engels and Lenin are divested of context and turned into incantation.

A complete analysis of this transition to magic on the part of a group who pride themselves upon their militant atheism would make a fascinating study, but such an inquiry is apart from the purpose of this brief work.

17

Whatever his particular work, the writer is a singular and lonely person. In the small hours of the night, tearing out of himself his particular story, he is perhaps more alone than almost any other person can be. He is the prisoner of his thoughts and fancies and visions, and he must struggle with them, capture them and order them into a structural whole. No matter how bad a writer he is, he is still a creature of conscience and is dedicated to the truth as he may see such truth within his own limitations; and no small part of his being less than a great writer is the result of limitations, both inner and outer, in his search for the truth.

To me, at least, it was neither surprising nor mysterious that the first bitter voices raised against the Communist Party tyranny in Hungary were the voices of writers; therein was the logic of my own existence and the existence of so many colleagues I had known well for long years; and therein was also the tragic and implacable dilemma of the writer in our time.

The simple crux of it is that the writer, as an artist, must perish under tyranny. I do not know whether the growth of literature as an art is a vital and necessary dynamic within a society of free men. I do know that it is the result of such a society; and I also know that when freedom is interdicted, literature shrivels and dies. Under a tyranny, the doctor can continue his practice of medicine; the carpenter can build houses as surely and precisely as before; and even the worker can continue to play his ordinary role in production. But from the writer tyranny demands the antithesis of his art, which is obedience.

In what came before, I attempted to demonstrate that the nature of Communist Party leadership was no accident of fate, but simply the logic of Communist Party history and organization. Neither is it through any accident of fate that the writer is drawn to the Communist Party, yet so often leaves it in despair, anger and frustration. The nature of the writer, embodied in his work, is compassion—not because writers as a breed are more compassionate than other people, but because the writer's day-to-day and year-to-year engrossment with the follies and hopes and dreams of human beings, as they relate within the social framework, must result in compassion to one degree or another. There are writers who are "hard-boiled," "objective," "indifferent," etc., but I know of no creative writer who has ever been able to free himself entirely from a certain amount of love and pity for the poor, damned creatures of whom he makes his stories—not even the very worst of writers.

In the light of this, it is perhaps less surprising that so many writers turn to the Communist Party. They see it the continuing logic of their existence as writers; out of man's mortal agony, they look for hope and social justice; and they see the Communist Party as a practical means of doing away with the oppression of man by man. Less easily do they come to understand that within the fanatical framework of obedience and discipline, they themselves must suffer—and eventually make the choice of giving up either the Party or all hope of growth and achievement as writers.

I have spelled out some of the circumstances that brought me to the point where I could no longer continue as a part of the Communist Party; but I have so far said nothing of a parallel process that must have led inevitably to the same conclusion—the matter of a writer's experience.

This is an experience that I underwent on two sides of the coin; for the problem of writing what I desired to write brought me the interdiction of two contending houses.

The effect upon me and the means used were not identical; for whatever capitalism does to the writer, it does not exercise the subtle process of destruction that is part of Communist practice, nor does it set up any single person as the high priest of decision. The entire literary history of capitalism is threaded through with writers whose writing was distasteful to the state power, but in the very process of their revolt against these influences, those writers gained enormous eloquence. Dickens, Dreiser and Zola come immediately to mind, and they are representative of a host of creative artists.

In other words, capitalism may visit its curse upon a writer, the writer retains the privilege of cursing and fighting back. Democratic capitalism cannot take hold of his very creative process and tear it out of him, offering death as his only alternative.

I state this explicitly because in what follows I put forward a certain balancing of the books—which is not to be taken as a comparison. In a democratic capitalist society, a great writer or artist carries the armor of tradition; even if he is not understood, his art entitles him to at least a degree of veneration. In the Communist structure, his art is despised —for all the large talk to the contrary—when he comes into conflict with the doctrine of the priesthood.

Let me underline this out of my own experience here in the United States. In my thirteen years of Communist Party membership, none of the national leaders of the Party ever discussed my writing except when I was brought before them on charges of violating the Party line. When I received the Stalin Peace Prize, Betty Gannett, then a member of the secretariat, cried out with anger, "Now he will be more difficult to control than ever!" No national leader of the Party, as a matter of fact, ever approached me except in terms of punishment or to ask me to attempt some task to his benefit. When Albert Maltz, in 1946, sent to the *New Masses* an article that contained a rather mild criticism of the narrow and sectarian Communist attitude toward literature, he was treated as if he had committed a major crime. I include myself among those who blew up his criticism all out of proportion to its intent—a matter for which I have never forgiven myself, even though Maltz found it so easy to forgive and forget. Meetings were held. Mike Gold denounced Maltz with passion and language that a civilized person would reserve for pathological criminals.

The fact that Albert Maltz was a writer of talent and unshakable integrity meant absolutely nothing. I myself have been denounced by writers in the general press as a "red" and as a "tool of Moscow," but Maltz was denounced by his own comrades as one seeking to strike a death blow at man's holiest hopes and aspirations. It was not simply that he had erred; he had sinned, and the aim was to make him submit to a process of total degradation. At that point, he had neither honor nor standing; and the Party leadership watched the process with approval and zest. For thus was the *line of the*

Party fought for and maintained, and if a human soul was crushed or maimed, it meant little.

Yes, the Party values its writers, but it has an inbuilt contempt for people, and writers are people.

Similarly, there comes to mind the case of Earl Conrad, who has written so much and so well in affirmation of the dignity of the Negro people. I do not know whether Earl Conrad was ever a Communist, and from all evidence I have he was not. But through his writing on the Negro he had gained a standing in progressive circles where Party people worked. Therefore, when his novel *Rock Bottom* appeared, the Party took criticism as its own task. It was not enough for the Party spokesmen to state that the novel departed from the Party line on the Negro question; they had to move on from there to attempt the total destruction of Earl Conrad, soul and mind, even as they had attempted the destruction of Albert Maltz. It was more difficult with someone who was not a Party member, but such was the influence of the Party where progressive writing was concerned that they were able to convince thousands that Conrad was a moral degenerate.

Those who recall this disgraceful incident will remember that I. F. Stone defended Conrad's book in the pages of the *Compass*, stating that he had read the book and found it to be one that definitely stood on the side of the angels. Who, knowing Conrad, could think otherwise? I found the book sincerely and forthrightly for social justice and equality, but when I spoke out in defense of Earl Conrad, I was myself threatened with expulsion. My own stature vanished immediately—and my few words in defense of Conrad brought such a torrent of suspicious hatred upon me that I might have then been the accomplished "counterrevolutionary" I am now called.

It is worth noting that then, in desperation, I gave the Conrad book to V. J. Jerome, the accepted Party commissar of culture, pleading with him to read it and form an independent judgment; but fear bulked larger in Jerome than justice or objectivity, and for weeks thereafter, until the issue had run its course, he bewailed the fact that he could not find time to read the book. Perhaps conscience made him tell me, a few years later, that he had intercepted and blocked a move to expel me from the Party for writing a suspense story called *The Fallen Angel*, a matter which I will go into later in this book.

Such was and is the attitude of the Communist Party toward creative writers and artists; it is parochial and contemptuous. Yet it would be unfair not to strike the balance. Within the non-Communist world, I was also shackled in my desire to write as I pleased.

18

As a member of the Board of the Joint Anti-Fascist Refugee Committee, I was one of those called before the House Committee on Un-American Activities, in that long past when it was under the leadership of Congressmen Wood and Rankin. A long-drawn-out process of trial and appeal finally ended with a prison sentence for contempt of Congress; for from the very beginning I, along with the other Board members concerned, had refused to surrender the record books and lists of names of people who had contributed to the work of the Anti-Fascist Committee and others who were helped by the Anti-Fascist Committee. I had felt, as a very simple matter of conscience, that when people put their trust in you to any extent, you do not surrender their names.

By the time I actually went to prison, my name had been coupled with the Communist Party many times; and while I never made any statement of membership in the Communist Party, I was equally careful to avoid any public denial of membership. The year before I began to serve my prison sentence—that is, during the summer of 1949, for I went to prison in 1950—the incredible riots centering around the Paul Robeson concerts outside of Peekskill took place. The events of these riots, about which I have written in some detail in a book called *Peekskill, U.S.A.*, again brought me into the public eye as a militant Communist. After this, in movement after movement, whether it was a struggle to save the life of a condemned Negro in the South or a campaign for Congress on the American Labor Party ticket, I found myself in the position of being—so far as writers went—more or less the public face of the Communist Party of the United States.

During this period I found my own destruction as a writer who had full and normal access to the American public. Bit by bit, that access was pared away; reviewers began to read Communist propaganda into things I had written; bookstores were reluctant to order my books; "public-spirited" individuals undertook movements to have my books banned; and *Citizen Tom Paine*, of all things, was thrown out of the New York City school system on the excuse of "purple passages." When I came out of prison in 1950, I undertook the largest, and to my way of thinking the most important, book of my career, *Spartacus*. When I had completed it, a year and a half later, I had come to the point where my destruction as a practicing writer in the stream of American literature was more or less complete. Seven leading commercial publishers refused to publish *Spartacus*. In despair, I published it myself—and, incidently, saw it become a best seller.

The above is of the greatest importance; to undertake to attack and reveal the Communist Party approach to writers and writing, while intimating that non-Communist America deals with literature entirely as a democratic nation might well and should deal with it, would be not only dishonest but deeply confusing. Other facts are more important; and for myself, the fact that a functioning democratic society is imperfect in its operative extension of democracy is not conclusive. We live in an imperfect world, a fact that men of good will have realized for centuries. They have tried to make this world better.

In the United States, I was crippled in my function as a writer. At great cost and financial loss, I had to publish my own books. From comparative wealth and success, I was reduced to a struggle for literary existence; and gradually my continuing work became less and less known.

But beyond deprivation, these facts are important:

1. I continued to write.

2. I continued to live.

3. I continued to fight for my inalienable privilege of writing as I pleased.

I spell them out like that because of the savage and unjustifiable experience of that time. I opposed the policies of my government and minced no words about it. I asked no quarter and gave no quarter; yet one, two and three, as specified above, were maintained.

My colleague in the Soviet Union, however, did far less than I in terms of his own government. He did not oppose it. He did not challenge it. At most, he dared to challenge within his craft. And concerning him, these facts are important:

1. He did not continue to write; he was silenced.

2. He did not continue to live: he was cruelly tortured and he was put to death.

3. He did not continue to fight for his "inalienable privilege of writing as he pleased." The privilege was alien to him; "as he pleased" was philosophically unknown to him, and when he tried to discover and embrace this unknown, his rulers rewarded him with death for the misfortune of plying his trade.

Were it not for the secret report and the mass of information from Communist sources that this report evoked and exploded, the above statement might be permissible but certainly open to grave question. It is one of those conclusions from life that appear to rest on no basis of logic or sanity, that is not relatable to the world outlook of the ordinary person. Not that we inhabit a world inexperienced in accounts of brutal and senseless murder; but the brutal and senseless murder of writers by government which purports to be socialist poses a contradiction akin to utter paradox and close to the edge of sanity.

In the same manner, many persons are at a loss to account for the world-wide resistance to communism now taking place among writers—the majority of them former Communists. Elsewhere in this book, I try to explain the forces which operate upon a writer to make freedom his professional as well as human necessity; but it is also important to see how the reverse of the process operated in Russia and the Eastern European countries.

We in the Western world have a far broader and more intimate knowledge of pre-Communist Russian literature than the Soviets care to admit. Not only were the major Russian novelists, such men as Tolstoy, Dostoevski and Gogol, prime influences in shaping the modern novel of today, but it is almost inconceivable to think of a thoughtful dramatist of our time as apart from the influence of Chekhov, a serious short-story writer who has not studied and admired the incomparable body of Russian short stories. If this is the case in the West, then how much more certainly is the writer in Russia and the East aware of his literary past!

There are many reasons for this splendid Russian literary flowering; I have space here to mention only a few in passing. The lateness of Russia on the modern scene, the sudden impact of the West and Western literature upon her small literate minority projected a sort of Renaissance situation into the nineteenth century, and apart from form, the sudden unfolding of Russian writing bears remarkable resemblance to the rich developments of the Renaissance. With this, a tradition of humanism among the ruling class was pricked into vital reformism by the constant political struggle against the tyranny of the Czar—and the awful extremes of wealth and poverty developed in a group of humane and thoughtful writers, a sense of compassion and concern with the dignity of man unmatched elsewhere in the world. The very fact that they could not be critical of their society, however this criticism was voiced, saved them from the platitudes and sentimentalism of their Western contemporaries and spurred them toward the highest perfection of the realistic method.

As with all great writers, they wrote not homilies but preachments, yet they did not preach; they bared, exposed, and carried on a relentless battle against hypocrisy, bigotry and cant. And this they did in a language which, to quote Lomonosov, includes "the magnificence of the Hispanic tongue, the sprightliness of the French, the sturdiness of the German, the *tendresse* of the Italian, and over and above all that, the richness and conciseness of powerful imagery of the Greek and Latin tongues."

Little wonder that they achieved something; but they also presented their Communist descendants with a problem. There is no use speculating on what literature might be in worlds we never knew; in human history, the best of literatures has been searching, impatient and critical. Sometimes, when the issues of the time when the literature was written are forgotten, the literature remembered, we tend to overlook the critical aspects; but even then the searching and inquiring nature of the work survives to give it what we call great-ness. So much is this the case that it defines literature; when you interdict the critic, the rebel, the prodding, bedeviling, annoying gadfly who disturbs, offends, irritates and provokes —then, you interdict literature itself. The two are one. There is no passive literature worth its salt, and so much does this appear evident that one hesitates to repeat it.

In other words, the simple practice of literature is *always* dangerous to tyranny; yet for a number of social and historical reasons, few tyrants murder their writers. One of these reasons is that the circumstances of tyranny usually prevent the tyrant from claiming total righteousness; another reason is that tyranny is rarely complete; still another, the relationship of the tyrant to world opinion; and again, and far from least important, the ever developing forces and traditions of civilization, which has always looked with a sour eye upon the persecution and murder of writers.

Russia provided the world with a new situation, the consolidation of power within the structure of power I have already described, the Communist Party. A great modern industrial complex was created within a nation that literally has no functioning government as we know government, but merely a framework of administration which the Communist Party controls with an absoluteness unmatched by any tyranny in all of human history. Elections, parliaments, courts, police, etc.—all the historically created mechanisms of balanced government exist only as devices for the Party to activate; and no part of this framework can even breathe without the will and consent of the Party. The formation of factions, other parties, areas of resistance, is almost impossible so long as the Communist Party can be maintained in its monolithic unity.

The result of this situation is sharply reflected in modern Soviet literature. The vitality of that literature in the 1920's reflected the pre-consolidation period of revolution and civil war, when the Communist Party in Russia was not yet large or secure enough to impose its will. The resurgence of vitality during the Hitlerite invasion of Russia was due to the fact that the people and the bureaucratic tyranny were for the moment united in the face of a single, overwhelming reality, the merciless advance of the monster of Nazism. Yet this resurgence never matched the original revolutionary vitality of the twenties; for in this war period, Russian literature shared the greatness of its past only when it dealt directly and exclusively with the enemy and the defense of the Soviet land.

For by this time, the basic privileges of the writer who would deal with reality had already been destroyed. The privilege—or, in the writer's sense, necessity—of criticism and opposition had already been removed; and in its place, as *reductio ad absurdum,* had been instituted the corruption of the original set of socialist ideals, dreams, and hopes. This consisted of a social method whereby, in the place of the only true morality, the morality of justice and the right to claim justice, there was substituted a set of "puritanical" dictums and injunctions, framed by the shoddy and limited understanding of the *commissars.*

Let me illustrate: instead of a forthright attempt to

change the condition of social degradation that has been the lot of the Russian woman, a series of *Victorian* bigotries concerning sex are adopted as the acceptable "reality," though they correspond not at all and influence in no way, the actual reality. But the actual reality is interdicted.

Instead of an intelligent attempt to understand the problems of youth, a description of youth directly out of the *Rover Boys* series of the early 1900's is adopted as norm and "reality." Again, this is not the reality nor does it influence the reality—but for the writer it is *law*. Under pain of severe punishment, he must accept it as reality.

Instead of a sincere attempt to understand America and Americans, their chewing of gum is equated with Nazism. Instead of facing the reality of the German worker, a "real" German worker is taken out of the writing of Lenin and set up as *being*. And so forth and so on.

But above all, the central reality which is interdicted is the fat spider which sits on the totality of Soviet life, the Communist Party and the commissar. The thin hope that the Party could possibly become humanized under the keen and devastating blows of observant and capable writers, plying their age-old task of speaking their piece with no hold barred, was utterly and finally shattered when Trotsky and the men around him were defeated, exiled and murdered. Thus, the writer was not only emasculated as an artist, but turned, by the very nature of his trade, into an incipient enemy of the Party.

And in this, the Party was right. I state it out of my whole life experience, observation, and conclusion—that as the Communist Party now exists, *every writer, no matter how dedicated and loyal he may appear, is potentially the enemy and destroyer of the Party,* moved by enormous forces which he can resist only to the destruction of himself as a writer of any worth at all.

When this is seen and understood, many things imperfectly comprehended in the past will become plain. The Communist Party of the Soviet Union destroyed Russian literature, not because the lords of the Kremlin would not like to boast of a great literature, but because the very defense of the Party and Party rule makes such destruction necessary.

The path can easily be traced by anyone who has the stamina and time to read through let us say a hundred Russian novels written since 1919. He will enjoy the freshness, vitality and excitement of the twenties and early thirties; he will be puzzled by the sudden descent into platitudinous mediocrity in the pre–World War II period; he will again be pleased and excited by a few war novels which emerge as works of vigor and achievement, such as Vassili Grossman's *No Beautiful Nights,* and Leonov's *Chariot of Wrath;* and then he will be disgusted and bored by the incredible spate of utter balderdash that follows the war and continues to the present day.

As a matter of fact, in a critical essay I wrote eight years ago to defend the Communist position in the arts, I was faced with this very sequence, and unable to explain it. But then, as yet, we had not seen the results of the postwar period in literature. I selected a lovely, haunting novel of the early thirties, Valentin Kataev's *Peace Is Where the Tempests Blow,* as a beginning point to show the concrete achievements of Soviet literature. Kataev's is a minor work, but excellent in every way, and together with Sholokhov's two heroic novels of the Don Cossacks, it made a reasonable beginning point. But when I sought to develop this, there was no place to go. I wrote to Russia, but they impatiently told me that Kataev wrote no more. He was "corrupt" and "lazy" and would not exert himself to write. About Sholokhov, they were vague and unspecific. The three or four other writers I inquired after were also "lazy." My Russian correspondents explained that the rewards of writing in their paradise were too enormous. Why should writers bother to work? This poised quite a problem.

The war produced great unevenness. When Simonov wrote about Stalingrad, which was Party business and political business as well as war, he produced the run-of-the-mill cops-and-robbers, Soviet version. Polovoy, in his *Story of a Real Man,* never presented even a hint of what was inside the "real man"; when we asked him personally, one evening at my home, how he had dared to write the incredible and priggish scene of the night in the home of the nurse, sex and love reduced to the Polly Pigtails level, he shrugged his shoulders, grinned sheepishly and explained, "Our people like it that way." But the stories of Sobolev, produced during and out of his personal war experience, contain many minor masterpieces, and Grossman's little novel ranks with the very best of our own war literature—still far below the best of the First World War.

But this very spasm of life and feeling served to highlight the literary meanness of the past decade. You would have to go a long way in America to find a book as bad as Sobko's best-selling Russian novel, *Guarantee of Peace.* A reader might be tempted to mention the vicious and immoral content of Mickey Spillane's books; and it is quite true that no such things come out of Russia. Spillane's books are one of the things a free society must endure, but America never lacked voices to spell out what they are, and as yet no one in Russia speaks bluntly and truthfully of work such as Sobko's. *Guarantee of Peace* has a high moral tone; everyone in the book behaves like the children in Mrs. Prim's Academy for Young Prigs; but the book is a disgraceful lie from cover to cover, and in that is a turpitude deeper than men and women kissing out of wedlock. The subject is occupied Germany, and the essence of the book's lies and perversions of reality is the same type of distortion as was practiced in describing the situation in Hungary before its revolution. Since that gem, I have sampled most of what the Russians translate into English, and you may be sure that in these translations they put their best foot forward; and I have found all of it to be cut out of the same cloth of bland distortion and Victorian priggishness—with three interesting exceptions, two of which were translated in foreign countries against the will of the Soviets.

But to get the total impact of the Soviet parade of current literature, one must read the books. Never—but never, in all of man's literary history, was a more incredibly boring body of work produced. There is no excitement, no conflict, no inner struggle of the characters, no outer struggle except to meet a *norm* or a *quota*. Hero and villain are absolutely pat, unchanging, identical regardless of writer or dramatic situation, and cut precisely to the pattern brought to perfection here in America by Horatio Alger and Nick Carter. Substitute *Party achievement* for *riches and wealth,* and you have it. It is not that these are bad books in the schoolboy sense; they all parade the fiction of Victorian morality, the basis of which was laid down by the bloody and paranoiac killer, Josef Stalin; they abound in copybook maxims and simple lessons on how to redeem one's soul. If you are my age, you will remember the *Rover Boys* and how the nasty villain always ended by turning over a new leaf under the influence of the sterling Rovers. Substitute sterling commissars.

Is it any wonder that, searching their souls in permitted areas, the Russian writers came to the conclusion not long ago that the production of good literature was no longer possible because the perfection of their society had eliminated conflict? Of course, you would think that after their war experience they would recall how Hitler eliminated inner conflict in Germany; but even if they had—where would they air such recollections?

The exceptions I mentioned are Ehrenburg's *Thaw,* a poorly written book, but nevertheless an attempt at reality by a writer long out of practice, the current *Not by Bread Alone,* which is constantly and officially attacked in Russia, and a delightful book of science-fiction stories by a scientist-writer called Yefremov; the only one of the three to receive the accolade of official Russian translation.

As to the first two books, they are the products of the impact of the Twentieth Congress in Russia itself, brief flashes of light if not of distinction, and welcomed hungrily by the Russian public. But the official hatchetmen of the Party have made it plain that this sort of dabbling in reality will not be tolerated in the future, and the Russian writers have harsh memories of what happens to members of their trade who provoke the temple gods beyond the point of toleration. I questioned every Russian writer or critic I met about Yefremov, and either they had never heard of him or they indicated that he was beneath their notice. In either case, he is fortunate—or perhaps the Politbureau finds itself baffled by the science-fiction future he depicts.

The other Eastern nations have given us nothing that I know of in translation—a startling fact after a decade and more of "socialist" culture. I may have missed a book or two here, for which I am ready to apologize—and diplomats from these countries who are interested in literature observe that there is so little if anything worth printing in their own language that one should not expect translation. The events in Hungary and Poland make this quite understandable.

So we have at least an indication of why the writer is put to death. In his own work, he lives with mathematical proof of the hole of horror in the promise he once idealized—and this proof makes him dangerous. Perhaps, in honor of an old and not inglorious profession, he will be dangerous enough to help topple the structure.

Is it strange that I make a case from writers, when I am a writer myself? I think not. Recently, after I had undertaken this work and finished the first part of it, the Soviet Union broke down the wall of silence that they had wrapped around me for so many months after I announced that I was no longer a Communist. Whatever their purpose was, they decided that I should no longer be the "man who never was," but Howard Fast, latest addition to the long list of those they term *renegades*. In the tirade that has become known as the "Soviet form of opinion" they charge me with borrowing, from anti-Communist propaganda centers, "false arguments and slanderous methods." I also repeat, according to them, the "inventions of . . . reactionary agents of Zionism."

In the Soviet lexicon of labeling and name-calling, a

"reactionary Zionist" is one who favors the continuation of the state of Israel as a refuge for persecuted Jews as well as a Jewish state. Since Russia is deeply involved in the power struggle for Middle Eastern oil, she looks upon any growth of Israel as a threat to her own aims. Thus it is not a simple question of incalling the Jews of other lands. The Soviet attitude toward the incalling of overseas Chinese is another matter entirely; and though these two cases are not wholly comparable, the whole Soviet attitude on the Jewish question is compounded of ignorance, bias, and latent anti-Semitism. To this date, no explanation of the utter destruction of Yiddish culture in the Soviet Union has been forthcoming, much less some comprehensible account of why the cream of Jewish writers and critics were put to death. Although both the Canadian and British Communist Parties have sent commissions to Russia to demand some explanation of this very matter, none has been forthcoming.

When I myself, in the pages of the *Daily Worker,* raised the question of the refusal of the Soviet Union to grant exit visas to any Soviet Jews, I characterized this as the mass imprisonment of a people. With the existence of Israel, this characterization raises problems never touched upon by the Communist movement before. Yet by all historical precedent, such is the fact.

With a thin veneer the Soviet spokesmen cover their anti-Semitism as they deliver the curse that should consign me to all the devils of hell. It is not conducive to objectivity for a writer to take the blows of his adversary as he writes. In the lexicon, "Zionist" means Jew, though there are good Jews and evil Jews, making a variant upon the simple racism of a Hitler. The evil Jews currently are the Jewish Jews, for if you take your position properly your ancestry is over-looked. And the great monster of a "Zionist" plot, which underlay their self-righteous slaughter of Jewish writers, is not new either. The infamous "Protocols of the Elders of Zion" are a good deal older than Khrushchev's rule, and one can say they have served even more unsavory masters. For twenty years I heard what Communists call "slanders" concerning the Soviets, but I refused to believe. If the power of belief is great, then I can assure you that the power of disbelief is equally great; and I did not wait for their bidding to say, out of my own conviction, not once but a thousand times,

"You lie in your teeth when you say this and that of the Soviet Union. These are slanders, hurled against the workers' republic by those who hate her and would see her destroyed."

But if I stand naked myself, seeing and learning that the "lies" were the truth, then let them not point a finger and dare to say that I betrayed them. I owed them nothing, and therefore I could not betray them; but to man's ancient dream of freedom and equality I owed a great deal, and this I betrayed out of an ignorance almost as awful as the truth.

It was Ignazio Silone who cried out so poignantly to the editor of the Russian *Literary Gazette*, in the recent exchange of correspondence between them, that if a poet were murdered by the government of Italy, the voice of the people's rage would rise like thunder. I do not know that as fact, for I do not know Italy; but in a land where poets and novelists can be tortured, beaten to pulp, and then executed in silent degradation, freedom is a stranger.

I asked about a certain Russian poet. All good writers are poets to one extent or another, but that is a way of saying something. It is something else and clearer, to say that the poet is a very special sort of writer; and when the poet is a great poet, his songs come as close to probing the meaning of human existence and human destiny as any human effort can. This poet I refer to was Itzik Feffer. It happened that some of us here in America knew him personally, for early during the war he came here on a good-will mission and he won our hearts. A tall, handsome man, wearing the uniform of a colonel in the Red Army, he appeared to be a symbol of what the Soviet Union had pledged in the way of wiping anti-Semitism out of Russia; for Feffer was a Jew, a beloved poet in the Soviet Union, an army officer, and a man who in every word he spoke breathed the love of his fatherland.

How then that the rumor came to us, a good while before the Twentieth Congress of the Bolshevik Party, that he was dead, and that he had died strangely? We didn't know. I asked and others asked,

"Where is Itzik Feffer and how did he die?"

A hundred times that question was asked and left unanswered, and we who asked it were looked at as fools because we could not understand the political subtleties of the murder of poets. I asked it of a *Pravda* correspondent, only a few days before I finally broke with the Party—but I was an unwelcome guest now in the beautiful building on Park Avenue, for I had already spoken my first angry criticism in the pages of the *Daily Worker* and the Communist cultural magazine, *Mainstream*. As the diplomatic reception eddied around us, this man from *Pravda*, talking with the voice of "socialism" and "brotherhood," said to me angrily, in English, which he spoke very well,

"Howard, why do you make so much of the Jews? Jews?

Jews? That is all we hear from you! Do you think Stalin murdered no one but Jews?"

I will go under oath that I quote him exactly and precisely, for while there are some words that eddy away like smoke, these were graven on my mind. When my children were small, we used to make what we then called jump-ups. We cut out paper figures and objects, and fastened them one behind the other to a sheet of paper. When the paper was unfolded, the recumbent figures popped up. So did a whole epoch pop up in his words—the word "Jew" turned into an epithet, the Brown Shirts of the Brown House of Berlin, the gas chambers and the slaughterhouses where green soap was produced from the body elements of murdered Jews. Yet to his retort I had no answer; there are memories that are meaningless if another must be reminded.

The Twentieth Congress came and went, and still a mocking, derisive silence greeted the question, "Where is Itzik Feffer and how did he die?"

But the death of a poet is not so small a matter as some think. A Pole, tears in his eyes, said that the wind was full of small voices; and bit by bit we put together the story of Itzik Feffer. After the Twentieth Congress, Communists went to Russia and Communists came back, and each had a little bit of the full story and a few a great deal of it. Perhaps this reconstruction of the story is not exact, but it is all I could find. It begins with the arrest of David Bergelson, the internationally famous Jewish-Soviet writer. Why he was arrested we don't know; only the Russians can answer that. But in all likelihood it was part of this "Zionist" invention, and the fact is that Bergelson was arrested because he was Jewish, whatever the other reasons were.

He was put in prison and systematically beaten so that he might confess to crimes concocted for him to confess to. No brainwashing, no truth serums, none of the science-fiction fantasies; just the truncheon and the whip and the heady injunction of Stalin, "Beat, beat, beat—and beat again."

Before Bergelson died, Itzik Feffer learned where he was and what was happening to him; and being a friend of his, Feffer set out to try to save him. Writer after writer refused to join with Feffer. They were afraid. They told Feffer that if he persisted he would be arrested. Feffer pleaded with Ehrenburg, and the story goes that Ehrenburg refused. Ehrenburg stood high and well with Stalin. The story also goes that Feffer cried out to Ehrenburg:

"Then I'll do it alone—and when they arrest me and kill me, my death will be upon your soul for as long as you live!"

As it was. Thus, because he was driven by his human conscience, Feffer perished with Bergelson. Where then was Fadeyev, who shot himself after the Twentieth Congress? Where was Polovoy, whom I loved and respected as I have loved and respected few men? Where was Simonov? Where was Sholokhov? Where were all of these who had lectured the world upon the honor and integrity of humankind—these "socialist" men? Where were the preachers and righteous ones of the *Literary Gazette*? Where were those Soviet writers of honor who called America a land of barbarians without a heritage or a culture?

Yes, we killed Sacco and Vanzetti, but our own cry went out to haunt the world. Was my own voice ever silent concerning injustice in my own land? In the name of all that is holy to you, my Russian colleagues, where were your voices when murder walked in your land? And today, the question of the poet remains unanswered.

In writing this, I am not shedding guilt. I take no refuge in the fact that I made my voice heard against injustice here. Joseph Clark, the foreign editor of the *Daily Worker* then, and before that Russian correspondent for the *Daily Worker*, sat in my living room in January of 1957 and cried out to me, in a tortured voice that only disguised his own heart-sickness and guilt,

"If you and Paul Robeson had raised your voices in 1949, Itzik Feffer would be alive today!"

Nor had I the spirit to claim that I did not know in 1949—even as one outside of Russia had then known that Feffer stood before the firing squad. For in a sense Clark was right in his accusation. But it is not with this failure to know, to believe, that my Russian colleagues charge me; not at all. They claim that I have betrayed them because I cannot remain silent.

Oh, lightly enough did we become writers in the beginning. We loved the sound of a story and the music of words, and we loved the books that we dreamed of making. There was no one to tell us that the desire would turn into a passion and the passion into a curse; and that eventually our obligation would be at odds with the whole world. Some of us learned, but with awful pain; for wherever we stood, we came to know that sooner or later we must break the image—for we had singled ourselves out to be enemies of obedience. It becomes a reversal of the old Faustian legend, for unless we spit in the face of the devil, in whatsoever form he be, we end with the barter of our souls.

I set out here in this section of what I write to make a

few comments on the writer as he stands today in society, the Communist Party on his left, the fleshpots of well-paid mediocrity on his right; but I make no judgments. I am past that, as regards my colleagues in this profession. I can only tell what happened and why I as a writer could exist no longer in the Communist movement. I no longer enjoy the practice of my craft; it is full of pain and too many memories, but it is all I know; and I don't ask that anyone should weep for writers. Ours is an old and once honorable craft, and perhaps someday it will be that again.

But I cannot love the Party for what it did to us—and not the worst was to the dead. The living were also naked. I am alive. Boris Polovoy is alive. We were comrades in a movement that I believed with all my heart and soul—he the head of the Union of Soviet Writers, myself a Communist writer in America. We came to know each other by correspondence, and through our letters a love and warmth and mutual respect grew and flowered. When finally I met him in New York, where he had come as the leader of a delegation of Soviet writers, I embraced him as a beloved and old companion. He was big, warm, open, his smile a thing of joy to see as my wife and I dragged him home with us. "No fear?" he wanted to know. "My coming to your home?" But how could fear exist when the two of us were together? We had rich lives to share; we had lived and seen and ventured a thing or two, and we were knit beyond politics, beyond continents, in that fine brotherhood of our craft. What an evening that was—of warmth and closeness and drink and food and fellowship!

We saw him again the following day, my wife and I, at a party given for himself and his comrades. Again the warmth, closeness and openness. Here were a round dozen of us, Russian and American, and our feeling was, "May the devil take politics and politicians too. We are together—may all the people of both our nations come to know each other, openly and in good friendship."

During the course of that evening I happened to be in a little group that was talking to Boris Polovoy. The conversation concerned Russian writers and what they were currently doing, and since Polovoy spoke no English, the translation was provided by an old friend of mine, a brilliant student of Slavic languages whose Russian was perfect. The faultlessness of his Russian was important, for I have since checked and rechecked this story as to accuracy. Someone asked Polovoy whether he couldn't provide us with some information concerning the Jewish writer Kvitko. He explained to Polovoy that for some time now, rumors had been circulating to the effect that Kvitko, among other Jewish writers, had been arrested and subsequently put to death. Could Polovoy settle these rumors once and for all?

Polovoy said that he could. The rumors were, of course, the usual anti-Soviet slanders. Fortunately, Polovoy said, he was in a position to refute them, for Kvitko was at present living in the same apartment house as he, Polovoy. Could there be a better denial of any rumor? he asked.

We were relieved and delighted. We asked what Kvitko was doing, and Polovoy said that he was finishing a translation and planned a new book after that. He also added that he had seen Kvitko before leaving for America and that he, Kvitko, had asked Polovoy to convey his very best regards to friends in America.

So Polovoy answered, and this was witnessed by too

many people that night to be denied. But after Polovoy had gone home, after the Twentieth Congress, we learned via a Jewish-Polish Communist paper that Kvitko had been dead for years, beaten and executed even as Feffer had been, even as Bergelson.

I say: May all the implacable justice of time and history be visited upon those who not only murdered men and artists, but who dirtied the soul of such a man as Boris Polovoy. For it was not merely that he told a tragic and grotesque lie; his invention was the summation of what the Communist Party does to a writer.

19

For me, a time, a life, a long thread of motion came to an end in the period after the Twentieth Congress. It would be both a lie and an act of unbearable priggishness for me to pretend that, during all the weeks and months I pondered Boris Polovoy's invention, I did not ask myself whether I might not have done the same thing in his place. Nor can I truthfully say that I know the answer to such a question; for, like Polovoy, I underwent a process. But the mind of man is a marvelous instrument, and it compensates for distortion of reality. From the very beginning of my Party experience, I, like so many others, began to accumulate a store of hatred. I say flatly that *there is no Communist of any integrity and intelligence* who does not accumulate such a store of hatred during his experience in the Party. For rebels do not take easily to obedience; they must be whipped into it, and a whip leaves scars.

I am not attempting here in any manner a story of my experience in the Communist Party; I am simply trying to silhouette a number of incidents that led to certain conclusions concerning the Party, and as a writer, I found these incidents were coupled with the commissar, whosoever he happened to be at the moment. He was the governor on my mind and my creative dreams. He was the checkrein. He was the "conscience" that the comradeship of the Party supplied. Myself extracted from my primitive knowledge of right and wrong, he would supply a knowledge of right and wrong that operated, to use that most precious of Party expressions, "on a higher level." In the Party, there was an endless variety of levels, zooming higher and higher and higher until at last one touched the exalted intelligence of Stalin. One touched it, and no more; for there were heights to which no other mortal climbed.

My own level was rather low, and there it remained for thirteen hard years. Fast was a good front, it was said, an able public speaker with a few other virtues, a knack for storytelling, but not "politically developed" to any great extent; and in the beginning I accepted this. My first meetings—the rapid and clever argumentation and quoting of "scripture," the skill of refutation—all of it left me a little bewildered and humble. The first commissar I met—he was the paid organizer of the section to which I was assigned —compensated for this very cleverly. A thin, slight, intellectual-looking man of about forty, he stressed his own humility and laid out for me two worlds of knowledge and skill. In the non-Communist world, he acknowledged my achievement and knowledgeability; in the Communist world, he emphasized his know-how. He explained very matter-of-factly that I would want and need either a crutch or a strong staff to lean upon, depending on how you looked at it. He was that. He also held that I would find a constant need for that element which is pronounced like the name of the holy of holies within Communist circles, to wit, "clarity." It was taken for granted that until now I had lived cheek to cheek with confusion; I could no longer afford this; it would be, in the private phraseology of the Party, "detrimental to my political development." It would be both his pleasure and duty to supply this much-needed "clarity."

It must be noted at this point how clearly this attitude, which every Communist will recognize, fits into my previous picture of the Party structure as a temple, the Party dogma as holy writ, and the functionaries of the Party as a priesthood. The layman was not capable of either reading the writ or acting in life in accordance with it; but that of course was not my reaction at the time. I was at the beginning of an experience, not at the end of it.

I saw only a personable man who with due modesty exhibited a vast store of knowledge concerning the organization with which I had allied myself; and myself, I knew no more of that organization than its name and stated purpose. Not for years to come would I begin to understand the working mechanism of it. At this time of which I write, my novel *Freedom Road* was completed, printed and bound, and scheduled for publication in the near future. I had given this section organizer a copy to read, and now he asked me for half a dozen additional copies.

He explained that the book presented problems. It was quite true that I had written the book before I joined the Party; nevertheless the problem was a difficult one. He did not want to see the Party attack me and the book so soon after my joining, yet he stressed the fact that the Party could very well make such an attack. The attack would fall into place under another holy expression of the Party lexicon, "principled action."

On hearing this I was sick and horrified—a feeling I would become increasingly familiar with as subsequent books of mine were published—and I begged to know what awful mistake I had made. He corrected me. In the Party lexicon there were no mistakes, only "errors"—"errors of judgment," "political errors," "errors of a bourgeois nature," etc. I had indulged in an error.

A misinterpretation of history, surely?

No, he said, my error was not a misinterpretation of history. My error was more serious. Throughout the book I had used the word *nigger*. This in itself constituted grounds for expulsion from the Party; and taken together with the fact that Mike Gold, writing in the *Daily Worker*, had seen in my previous novel, *Citizen Tom Paine*, certain Trotskyite tendencies, it could give rise to a very serious situation. Not that he agreed with Mike Gold. He, the section organizer, presented himself as a man of sound common sense, and he stated bluntly that Mike Gold was a damn fool about such things. But there it was.

I attempted to justify my use of the word. I made it plain to him how utterly despicable I regarded it as a descriptive word, but held that since the word was used at the time of which I wrote just as I had used it in the book, how possibly could I avoid using it? The whole matter of *plausibility*, so important to a creative writer, would be undermined; and what hope was there for me to capture the reader's attention and belief if I engaged in anachronisms and contrivances? And in any case, the book had been printed in a very large edition, and at this point there was nothing I could do about it.

He acknowledged the discussion after the fact, but no more. I was engaging in bourgeois premises and missing the whole point of a "socialist realism," to the elevation of "naturalism." It was true that in certain instances of direct quotation, the Party permitted the use of n——r, but never the spelled-out word. However, all was not lost. He had, he let me know, certain powerful and reasonable friends who were high in the Party apparatus; he would give each of them a copy of the book to read; and if they threw their weight into the picture, an exception might be made in this case.

I may say that his political know-how was effective, and though by the skin of its teeth, *Freedom Road* was well spoken of in the Communist Party press. I had crawled through the first barrier.

All this in spite of the fact that *Freedom Road* subsequently sold almost two million copies and was taken to the hearts of the Negro people as was no other novel of our time. The measure of joy and hope and pride it gave to Negroes was of no consequence when set against my violation of a specific Party insanity. In its frenetic struggle against what it was pleased to call "white chauvinism," the Communist Party of the United States performed a series of actions amazingly similar to those of its brother party in Russia. It engaged in a wild witch hunt based on symbolic taboos and became so engrossed with this magical exercise that it abandoned the fight for Negro rights and lost all mass support among the Negro people. This lunatic procedure continued to a point where Communists who had given years of their lives and risked death over and over in the struggle for Negro rights were themselves characterized as more evil than the Ku Klux Klan. A dear friend of mine, who had spent years of danger and privation as a Party organizer in a Southern state, who could no more offend a Negro than he could jump over the moon, was told by Pettis Perry that he was more racist than Bilbo.

People were expelled from the Party for speaking of a "Negro girl" or of a "black night," for both "girl" and "black" had become magical taboo words, the use of which indicated that a white person had deep wells of racism within him. This particular horror mounted to a point where dozens of Communists I knew avoided the company of all Negroes, so terrified were they of taboo words or actions that could lead to expulsion. Work among the Negroes collapsed completely, and at last William Z. Foster had to step in to halt what was becoming a threat to the very existence of the Party itself. Many Party members had this grotesque memory in mind when they read the Khrushchev report.

One should also note here the use of n——r in Party publications instead of the word "nigger." Of course this is a distasteful and offensive word, and so are other words, but they are a part of social-historical reality. What nonsensical prudery is served by leaving out the middle letters? But this is typically the level of morality, when such "original" morality is developed out of the Communist movement and it is less than consistent. Kike, sheeny, wop, waug, spick —all of these equally vile epithets are spelled out, for the Russians are easygoing, to say the least, on the Jewish question, and the other nationalities have failed to press their sensitivities.

Now, since the specific has been cited, it is the turn of the reader, who will unquestionably ask, "How in heaven's name did Howard Fast, a man of at least some intelligence, allow himself to be subjected to this ridiculous charade? Why didn't he turn around and walk out as he had come in?"

The answer is not so simple. For the first time, I said to myself what I was to say again and again during the coming years: "I joined this movement because I am an anti-Fascist and because I believe in peace and socialism. On this question, which is a question of writing, I think they are wrong. I am not going to run because of this bit of nonsense."

I said the same thing again and again and again as the years rolled by. I reached a point where, like so many other Communists I knew, I began to take a perverse pride in the fact that I could not be broken, that I could maintain my sanity, and that I could avoid expulsion from the Party. The commissars changed as the years passed, but the nature of the insanity did not change. The strength I exhibited is nothing to be proud of, and the fact that I was reduced to a point where I scanned each manuscript microscopically in hope that I could frustrate the end critique is utterly contemptible as I look back upon it. My only virtue lies in that I continued to sin.

In those years the commercial press of America brushed me off as one who writes Communist propaganda; the Communists brought me up on charges; I sat in the middle—*as did every other creative writer of any talent who was a Party member*. And if the whole truth be told, I suffered less than certain others, for I had at least a long-established position in the non-Communist world and an international reputation that was particularly strong in Russia. This, at least, acted as a brake; for a Russian critique of one of my books carried weight. There were other Communist writers who had no such "protection," and more than one of those were destroyed, spiritually and creatively, from within the Communist Party.

Of them, there is little that I can write here; for what I wrote would have small meaning unless I named names, men and books; and that is impossible without bringing additional suffering to people who have endured sufficient.

Yet with all my "protection," the process went on. There is a notion current that Communist writers are told what to write, but this contains as little truth as most of the popular legends about the Party. There are two reasons why this is impossible. Firstly, the Party leadership have neither the wit nor the power of imagination to contrive content for any novelist; and secondly, even they recognize that such a procedure would make writers nonoperative.

There is another popular notion that Communist writers must submit manuscripts to be read before publication. In all fairness, I must say that no one in the Party leadership —with the single exception of Steve Nelson, a very wonderful human being who was never admitted into the top leadership during my years—ever showed the slightest interest in what I was writing or in reading any manuscript of mine before publication. In my case, interest came only when my "bourgeois literary sins" were unearthed by the specialists in the field and then brought to the attention of the leadership. Yet I have known many writers who, of their own free will and sense of discipline, submitted their manuscripts to be read by so-called "cultural" leaders of the Party. I have seen such manuscripts savagely torn into critical pieces, dogmatized and robbed of essence until the writer, beaten and hopeless, reduced his work to the lifeless husk the Party demanded. In my own case, quite by accident, a manuscript of a play of mine entitled *30 Pieces of Silver* fell into the hands of a petty Party functionary. It was given to him by an actress when he asked to read it. After he had read it, he called me on the telephone, demanded that I come to a certain place to meet him, and there arbitrarily, in terms of savage vindictiveness, ordered me to change the third act of the play. He told me quite bluntly that he was very close to Pettis Perry, then general secretary of the Party, and that unless I made the changes he demanded, he would see to it that Perry expelled me from the Party. He also let me know that Perry would in no way be displeased to have an excuse for taking that action. I made the changes.

The reiteration and itemization of this type of thing is both degrading and boring; yet for all the mean and sordid humiliation of the process, I can say, looking back now, that I think I did right through those years in refusing to allow myself to be expelled from the Party. If I had allowed it to come to that, as so many others did, I would have lost all power to influence the hundreds of thousands the world over who today see themselves in much the same position as myself.

Yet it was no easy task. When I published my novel *Clarkton,* I was charged with anti-Party action because I had depicted an Irish worker, a Communist, as taking on a bit of a load when his problems became too great for him.

When *My Glorious Brothers* appeared, I was brought up before the secretariat of the Party on charges of Jewish bourgeois nationalism. It had become a bitter jest in Party circles that all nationalism can be both admirable and a progressive stage in the development of a people except Jewish nationalism. Jewish nationalism is anti-Party, anti-Soviet, anti-progressive. Irish nationalists are heroes, but Jewish nationalists are the "running dogs of imperialism."

Arab nationalists are patriots ranged against oppression; Jewish nationalists are tools of the oil interests, even though oil abounds in the Arab lands and is more or less absent in Israel.

Since *My Glorious Brothers,* a tale of the great agrarian war of the Jews under the Maccabees, obviously fostered Jewish nationalism, the Russians solved the problems of the moment by simply refusing to recognize that I ever wrote it. It was never mentioned or reviewed in the Soviet Union, much less published; and even when Russian scholars prepared authoritative bibliographies of my work, including obscure articles I wrote for American publications deceased these many years, they carefully omitted *My Glorious Brothers.*

When *The Proud and the Free* appeared—it was a novel of the American Revolution—I was brought up before a special meeting of the secretariat, then consisting of Betty Gannett and Pettis Perry, with V. J. Jerome added as special cultural consultant. This time I was charged with white chauvinism, most seriously, and given to understand in no uncertain terms that unless I made satisfactory public apology, I would be expelled from the Party.

I have always had a particular affection for *The Proud and the Free.* It was the last book of mine during that period to be brought out by a commercial publisher of established standing. It was published in the fall of 1950 by Little, Brown. Understandably, it received little public attention then, at the high point of both the Korean War and McCarthyism. Yet, at the risk of being decidedly immodest, I will say that I feel it to be one of the best novels on the

American Revolution to appear in recent years, superior to my other novels of that same period, and certainly the most lyrical work of my whole lifetime. In it I attempted to catch the essence of revolution, to bare the eternal soul of the revolutionary as symbolized by the poor glorious devils of Anthony Wayne's Pennsylvania Line, and in that way to create my own song and symbol of America. On the basis of years of research, of listening with a not unskilled ear and of intimate association with people who still speak the language of our ancestors, I attempted to re-create the speech of that time and to achieve at least something of what only Conrad Richter among our living writers has attained.

How well or poorly I succeeded, I hope that someday more impartial critics than those who judged the book originally will decide; but even my attempts were of no interest or importance to the three who sat in judgment upon me. They were concerned with the original sin that marked my entrance into the Party, for here I had used the eighteenth-century word "nayger" for Negro, putting it on the lips of Colonial soldiers who actually used it. For that, I had to write a public confession, apology and degradation —which would appear in the pages of *Political Affairs,* along with the additional confession on my part that I had made the soldiers of the time too knowledgeable, since in doing what they did they violated cardinal principles of "Marxist" revolutionary development.

But this I could not do. Seven years had passed since the first incident, and I had come to understand a good deal better the nature of this sickness. Whether I would have accepted expulsion from the Party then, I do not know;

ironically enough, I was saved, if one wants to call it that, by government action against *Political Affairs* and its editors. It was conceded that at this moment it would be unwise for me to appear in the magazine with a confession of this sort; and a year and a half later, when the issue might have been raised again, a new culprit had appeared on the scene, this time my novel *Spartacus*.

20

I think that only another writer can understand what went into the making of *Spartacus,* a book I had dreamed of writing for years. I developed it in my mind and gave it structure, so as to speak, in a Federal prison. Outside, I sat down to write a trilogy of twelve hundred pages, wrote and pruned for a year and a half—and emerged finally with five hundred fifty manuscript pages and the sense, for the first time in my life, that I had mastered my material and created an enduring book. As I read it over, all that I had written in the twenty years before this time seemed immature, half-finished. That was not a considered judgment; it was merely that I was flushed with the gratification of having licked the hardest job I had ever undertaken as a writer and also produced something of worth.

The book was submitted to seven publishers, all of whom declined to publish it—and at that point, unable to endure the humiliation of further rejections, I decided to publish it myself. So it began—the editing, printing, packing, distributing, and finally the miracle of a book published by myself turning into a best seller and selling thirty-five thousand copies in a few months.

But the commissar knew I had sinned and must be punished for my sins. This time he was the "cultural overlord" of the West Coast, at the moment in New York, and he was filled with hate and anger for the book I had written.

My own stupidity was inexhaustible; my own inability to learn was beyond correction. For two years and more I had labored to produce a book that would be an epic of the oppressed, a paean to liberty and the high conscience of mankind. I had labored under the notion that I was furthering and giving more complete expression to the values that had guided my life. But the lashing tongue of the commissar informed me otherwise.

I had written a study in "brutalism" and "sadism," two words that he used over and over. He said to me, in no uncertain terms, "I think it is a bad book, an evil book, a rotten book!" And then he turned to V. J. Jerome, who was standing and listening, and cried, "I think, Jerry, that we must attack this book and denounce it! I think that we must not hold back in this case! I think this book must be destroyed. It is a rotten book."

Jerome will remember the incident well. There was to be no arena of discussion, review, criticism. I was judged guilty, but in contradiction to certain legal situations, I was not even to be given an opportunity to prove or attempt to prove my innocence.

Another charge directed against *Spartacus* was that it contained psychoanalytical words. This charge was made by a Party member who actually played the role of a one-woman literary *Ogpu*. It was her work—self-appointed but in time semi-official—to search books for the more subtle type of deviations. The phrase "inner struggle" in particular was seized upon, as well as a number of other words. This example of a seemingly innocuous process of attrition becomes in effect the most destructive type of writer control.

Yet it turned out in the end that they could not destroy *Spartacus*. The petty shame of Party periodicals rejecting reviews they had asked to be written because these reviews praised the book was drowned in the excitement of Communists who read it—and it sold through edition after edition. Power the commissars had, but it was limited to the structure of the Party, and that structure was already beginning to shake.

Yet that night I could hear only one thing—that my life and work and talent, as embodied in that book, had to be destroyed. I had sinned, disobeyed, created as I thought I should create—and all that was criminal. The commercial book publishers of the United States had hustled me out of their offices because I was a Communist; the Communist Party had established its discipline because I was a writer. I sat down that night and wept, because it was the end.

But even if that night, when my defeat as a writer, a creator and an artist appeared to me to be complete and total, I had only tasted the particular cup of bitterness. It was as if the Communist bureaucracy had decided that the case of *Spartacus* was the line on which the battle with Fast must be fought to a finish. They were never those to savor literature, to know its nuances and subtleties; but I do think that on this occasion they sensed a deep truth—that in the life of every writer, there is one work that he will someday write out of the bottommost wells of his passion and knowledge and human experience. For me, then and now too, *Spartacus* was such a book—the book of my own being.

To make what happened plain, I must tell a little of the book's story; and it is worth doing so, for it goes to the crux of Communist censorship and criticism. Spartacus, you will remember, was the Thracian slave and gladiator in ancient Rome who led a mighty slave revolt that almost overthrew Rome itself. Very little is known of Spartacus or the men in his army, so most of the story had to be a creation on the base of the few facts I had. Among these was the story of Varinia, wife of Spartacus, and of the deep love between them. Varinia was said to have been taken captive from one of the Teutonic tribes—then at a stage of development not much further advanced than our American northeastern woods Indians at the time of the white man's coming.

Though the book I wrote was a combination of symbolism and realism, I devoted great fidelity to the historical scene, attempting to achieve the utmost values of truth and plausibility at least in general. No one knows what happened to Varinia after the death of Spartacus, so I took the liberty of creating a psychological situation where, to the two most important Roman characters in the book, she became the mysterious symbol of what their lives most lacked, purity and integrity. One of these two Romans, Crassus, the aristocratic general, achieved the final destruction of Spartacus —but found his victory hollow unless he could possess Varinia through her own consent. He takes her to his home in Rome. The other Roman, Gracchus, politician, leader of the Roman proletariat, low-born, but brilliant and ruthless, led the political struggle against Spartacus. The two men destroyed the slave leader, but they hated each other. Gracchus operates under the compulsion to deprive Crassus of Varinia—even to the extent of giving her freedom and making it possible for her to escape to the North. So great is his pride, so keen his sensibilities, so fat and gross his physical form, that the very thought of her recoiling from him makes him repress all desire to have her; he asks only that she spend a few hours talking to him, that she explain to him the enigma of his own life—Spartacus.

In those hours, Varinia succumbs to the enormous charm and personality of Gracchus—not physically, but in the sense of knowing a totally different man from Spartacus for the first time—and realizing the humanness and quality of him, for all that he was the mortal enemy of her dead husband. Understanding that Gracchus will face death at the hands of Crassus if he remains in Rome, she begs him to come with her, to share her gift of liberty. He refuses. Varinia kisses him—the kiss one gives to a man who has chosen to die for your own freedom—and then leaves Gracchus to the fate he chose for himself.

To me, there was great and true importance in this scene, and without it the book would have been meaningless. Without the strange and complex virtue of Gracchus, ancient Rome is meaningless, her glory unexplained, her manifold nature, so rich and wonderful, consigned to the definition of Edom. Through the long months of writing, I had come to love and respect Gracchus. What a man he was! What courage, what dignity, what force, and what love of the truth, bitter or sweet, resided in his gross body! Even his name was symbolic and true, for as the Gracchi were the virtue of Rome, so also was fat Gracchus, the politician, who inherited from the Gracchi's downfall.

And even more deeply, Gracchus was the rare great politician of the American scene who, for all his corruption, never severs the strings that knit him to the people. Now, this was in the book, plain for any reader with an ounce of discernment to see—just as most readers recognized the simple validity of Varinia's response, the response of a tribal woman who is given that thing without which she must perish, her freedom. It was, to hundreds of readers I heard from, a fine and dignified symbolic study—and in the name of man.

But not to the commissars! To them, in terms of this scene I describe above, I had sinned beyond the totality of all my previous sinning. I had exalted a "capitalist beast," namely Gracchus. I had degraded a pure "Communist woman, a woman of the oppressed toilers," namely Varinia. I am not exaggerating; I am not burlesquing; I am describing precisely what happened. Listen to this, from the definitive review in the *Daily Worker* of February 17, 1952:

> What is intended here? Is this Goethe's idealistic vision of the Eternal Woman, leading us all, oppressor and oppressed, "upward and on"? . . . Fast's conclusion is not believable, either as art or as philosophy. It is true that individuals from a decadent class can press beyond their class into the higher realm of the advancing class . . . but it is straining artistic credibility and our sense of history that this should take place in the form of a search for human-sexual fulfillment by the two figures who symbolize the entire Roman decadence, the murderer of Spartacus and the gangster-politician. What we have here is a reverse from the class theme. . . . Can we imagine a Nazi pleading for the love of a Rus-

sian woman? . . . we get something very close to the
sexual reconciliation of the classes. . . . The incursion
is felt here . . . of the destructive influence of Freudian
mystifications concerning the erotic as against the social
basis of character. . . .

There should be no temptation to laugh. The ridiculous
is also hideous in this case, and I pasted the review into
my scrapbook alongside the anti-Communist reviews which
sneered at my "Marxist Rome" and my "comic book" charac-
ers. But I had not written my book for their praise. I was
understandably an anathema to them—but what of my own
comrades in whose cause and struggle I had written? Criticism—yes, I wanted it, I needed it desperately—but in all my
years in the Communist Party I never received a paragraph
worth being called honest and thoughtful criticism, only the
type of mumbo-jumbo printed above alternating with equally
ridiculous and thoughtless praise which shamed me by describing me as the "greatest" this and the "greatest" that.

I spare the author of this particular review the use of
his name, for I know only too well the agony and shame of
his existence today; and I also refrain from mentioning the
editor of the Communist magazine who rejected a requested
review because it failed to attack and destroy. For months
another editor, a dear friend of mine, failed to publish any
review, torn and distraught because he was afraid to do
otherwise than follow the commissar line on the book. For
hours, he begged me to understand his predicament. How
well I understood it—even as I understood his publishing
anti-psychiatry articles in his magazine when he himself

secretly reverenced psychiatry and understood full well what miracles it had wrought. But in the end, he published an even more vicious and eerie review than had appeared in the *Worker*. Now I had slandered Negro womanhood also, for were they not the most oppressed?

So it went. "Would our Communist women behave as Varinia had?" So it went, and I have little cause to complain. I did not leave the Party. As I had sown, so did I reap. But whatever it was inside of me that had given my work an excitement and passion that people loved came to an end.

21

I wrote other books after that and published them my-self and lost a great deal of money—all the money I had saved—sharing the experience of other writers who became their own publishers. They were well-written books, pro-fessional, competent, as befitted a man who had worked two decades and more at his profession, and they were *safe* books. The spark of life and the flame of passion were gone from them, but they were well scrutinized and free from the dread thing called "error." They were without song or fancy, but they obeyed the writ of the priesthood. They were well received by the leadership, who never bothered to read them.

Yet it would be entirely wrong to conclude, from any-thing I have indicated here, that the Party has simply a nuisance attitude toward the writer. Quite to the contrary, the Communist Party has a rich historical awareness of the role and importance of the writer, regarding him as an indispensable ingredient of the movement and a potentially dangerous enemy at one and the same time.

Even the Party writer becomes steeped in this attitude, and when he combines it with the problems he faces as a writer in the Party, he comes in time to mistrust himself. Like a talented yet untrustworthy child, he is alternately praised and disciplined in excess.

His first injunction is in the supposed language of Stalin —one of those ritualistic bits of wisdom that the Party is so fond of. He is told that, in the words of the master, "The writer is the engineer of the human soul."

The fact that I, for one, do not believe that Stalin ever wrote the phrase is unimportant. Heaven only know how much of Stalin's writing was penned by him, and it matters little. The point is that the credo was adopted. That it was utter nonsense, put forward by a man who denied the existence of a human soul, was something we never dared to express; and this unwillingness was cushioned by the extravagant praise that the apothegm directed toward the writer. There is no gainsaying that it is pleasant to think of yourself as a shaper of human souls—but it also has its maniacal implications.

Yet it is precisely through attaching this magical significance to the written word that the Party succeeds in obtaining the submission of the writer. In the normal course of events, in a normal world—or at least in a non-Communist world—the professional writer does not dwell inordinately upon the soul-shaping or earth-shaking importance of his work. He operates as a craftsman, creating good or bad work according to the situation and to his ability. If he lives within a tyranny, his work is circumscribed and he is punished for defying the powers that be. In the Communist Party, however, his work is haloed with mystical significance. He is no longer a working writer but an engineer of the human soul; he is the arm of the power or the enemy of the power. Laughter and spontaneity are frowned upon. The joy of writing for sheer entertainment is gone through interdiction.

Nowhere is the theoretical investigation of the process of creativity more sedulously probed than in the Communist Party, and nowhere are the results more sterile. I was not a knowing observer of this process, and I can claim no superior stand; indeed, if the process had not engulfed me, there would be little point in my argument—and my critical expositions during that period bore the trade-marks of the same frigid and deadly narrowness and intolerance that other Party material contained.

It was only my deep personal affection for H. L. Mencken that kept me from the stupid slanders against the man perpetrated by Mike Gold and others; and so with Eugene O'Neill and others who were mocked and derided by Mike Gold, John Howard Lawson, V. J. Jerome and so many others—because, forsooth, they were men of imagination and fancy. If I avoided the mindless attacks on these particular men, I in turn attacked others—for as I writhed under the barbs of my "comrades," I sought salvation in the exhibition of my own power to impale. I divided my mind and my soul; regardless of the souls of others, my own took a substantial licking.

I recall in particular one event that makes a point. In 1949, already feeling the effect of the blacklist, I decided, in the interest of making a living, to write a novel under a pseudonym. I wrote what Mr. Graham Greene calls "an entertainment," and I thoroughly enjoyed doing it. I wrote it lightly but not pointlessly, for it was a parable of the fears and tensions of this atomic age; and for anyone who is interested, it was titled *The Fallen Angel*. The first publishing house to which it was submitted accepted it, but certain events revealed my name as the author to the publishers, and subsequently they became so nervous about publishing me under a pseudonym, and about the thought of certain accusations that might be directed against them, that they decided to put my name on the inside dust-wrapper flap.

Not only did this cause trouble for the book in the commercial market, but inevitably, the Party harpies seized upon it and brought against me the whole gamut of charges. For here, writing in secret, all my concealed "bourgeois" evil tendencies emerged.

The grotesque humor of the situation is less than humorous to the writer involved. For the writer, his own mental and moral destruction is far from humorous. And at the end, as in my own case, he must face the fact that the process was his own doing. Among the great tragedies of mankind, his own is minor and muted.

22

So it was done. It is by no means the whole story of my life in the Communist Party, but I doubt that I will ever write that story or even desire to. It is not an experience that one cares to dwell upon overmuch. People who turned to this essay for what is commonly thought of as sensational disclosures will be disappointed, for there are no sensational disclosures here and nothing about the so-called "Communist conspiracy." So far as I am concerned, out of a knowledge I paid a price for, there is no Communist conspiracy in the terms paraded by the sensation-mongers and the professional anti-Communists. A senseless fabrication has been used to cover a truth more terrible and damning than these dream merchants could ever create—the truth of what there is, the Communist Party.

We who are writers have had a peculiar and singular experience with the Communist Party, and I have given you here a brief outline of my own. In that you have seen a strange development—and perhaps a terrifying one for people of imagination. One of the cardinal tenets of the Protestant Reformation was the recovery and redevelopment to new heights of the ancient Judaic-prophetic creed of the individual's responsibility to his own soul and to his own conscience. The Jew in his development of prophetic monotheism—and I talk here of social rather than religious evolution—put forth the concept of a covenant between man

159

and his God. This covenant or contract is central to prophetic Judaism; and among other things, it places responsibility for his own actions squarely upon the individual, making matters of social responsibility things which he himself must decide and act upon, such decision being lawful and acceptable in the eyes of God.

The re-examination of this concept by militant Protestantism marked one of the great forward steps of Western culture; for it took certain values or ethics that had come into being, historically speaking, out of the struggles of oppressed people against tyranny, and turned these values and ethics into permanent qualities of conscience. No human being is born with a conscience; a conscience is developed as a matter of national, community, group and family experience; and when this body of ethical experience derives from man's age-old struggle against oppression, slavery and injustice, it is humanistic, wedded to life and mercy and justice, and pledged to ever broadening horizons of human freedom.

There is a long and proud history of revolution to mark man's stages through history and up the ladder of social evolution; but until the Bolshevik revolution, each one of these stages exhibited a certain broadening of personal freedom. This was of course most marked in what Marxists call the "bourgeois revolutions." The Bolshevik revolution, however, specified a narrowing of personal freedom as a means toward the end of complete and ultimate personal freedom—a proposition developed in the theory of the dictatorship of the proletariat.

Throughout this book, I have raised the question of whether such a contradiction between the nature of the *means* and the nature of the *end* can exist. I do not think so.

The commissar is "Big Brother," and his role, in the deepest sense, is to replace the responsibility of conscience. He predicates a situation where the very nature of right and wrong has changed, and he denies the further ability of the individual to distinguish right from wrong as a matter of conscience. In his final stage, he obliterates conscience and substitutes his "holy writ" as dispensed by his own priestly function. The hellish nightmare that this can and must lead to is spelled out in the Khrushchev secret speech; for where the individual is robbed of conscience, the society of which he is a part must of necessity be robbed of both ethic and morality. The yardstick of judgment disappears, and right and wrong lose all historical meaning and significance.

The same movement that once, in its time of conscience when itself suffered oppression, swore an oath to do away with capital punishment for good and all, now laughs at its former pledge. Murder is no longer right or wrong, it is only necessary or unnecessary—and so it is with torture, freedom of speech and all phases of social justice. But the bitter jest, the devil's jest itself, lies in the fact that only the historically developed human conscience reflects the broadest necessity of mankind—and it is this very basic necessity, as mirrored in the human conscience, that the Communist Party rejects.*

* One of the important definitions of Karl Marx was that of freedom—which he defined as being embodied in the recognition of necessity. It is this recognition which spurs men toward changing and improving their social conditions. However, throughout the Khrushchev report and throughout many of the apologias presented for that report, there runs the implication that the itemized butchery can be explained by an overzealous recognition of the necessity that faced the Soviet Union in terms of foreign aggression. This corruption of Marx to dogma, the extinction of freedom in the name of freedom (magic ritual), is typical of the degeneration of such thinking.

The lesson is not only to them but to us; for we too, in our own way, are self-righteous. The whole world and all of man's hopes and dreams and civilization lies poised between these two self-righteous giants, and if we differ fundamentally, there are all too many ways in which we are the same. We have developed and clung to certain legal avenues for the democratic process; Russia has not; and the power-drunk lords of her Communist Party will go only when the people can endure them and their Oriental temple of organization and their dogma-ridden priesthood no longer. Yet that time will come.

Only our own stupidity can unite them.

This, then, is part of the conclusion of writers who were Communists. We moved toward a legend and illusion of freedom, brotherhood and hope, and when we discovered its meaning, we had to fight it. My colleagues lie dead in many lands, and perhaps it will seem for a long time that all they wanted was to make a poem out of their own notion and fancy. For this they had to die; and since death is always terrible, always final, always the ultimate, it may be that we will learn some day that the reason equates with the price.

And while my own brief story here may seem tiresome, even though it is such a small part of the whole, it has a reason for being and a deep meaning too. The endless slights, hurts, indignities and broken hopes that a person like myself endures in the Communist Party are of small moment. They would make intriguing chatter for a gossip column, but I am not interested in that. Only to the point is the brief history of how the priest-commissars functioned to destroy me as a writer.

Yet they failed. They failed with every writer of stature

and integrity who was ever a member of the Communist Party of the United States. Lacking the firing squad and the truncheon, they failed the world over—and even in the lands they ruled, the writers were not docile. As with us, so with other people. The writer's conscience is the matrix of his art, and he pays a special price when he surrenders it. But all people pay a price, as we must come to understand.

Yet we must also understand that the Communist writer pays for his resurgence, even as he paid for his initial doom. Thus he pays twice, and each time he gives a piece of his life away.

I think of that evening in New York in 1946, that we, my wife and I, spent with Alfred Kantorowicz—his last evening in America before he returned to the Soviet zone of Germany. The evening was very precious to us. Again and again, we had wanted to meet Kantorowicz, but always something had intervened. Now he was going home.

It was symbolic and wonderful—the German anti-Fascist writer, the veteran of the Spanish Civil War, the exile whose exile was over at long last—"Homeland, you'll be ours again" —the tired, thin man, his face so deeply lined, his eyes still burning with the hope they had never lost. Was it any wonder that, in song and story and drama, this man had become the strange, lonely, tormented yet noble hero of our time! The song originally was his song, and the whole world had come to know it and be a part of it—"But for us, there is no surrender!"—no surrender, ever, and now he was going home.

We talked and talked, and the hours passed. There was a note of pity, of muted love, in all he said—for in our America the first notes of repression were being sounded, and he was going home, as he believed so firmly, to socialism's triumph, to equality and justice and the ultimate of democracy. But we were left here, with the future unmade.

So we believed—and it was easy to believe when the premise was firm and one could still set aside the mockery of the human spirit. But as the years passed after 1946, the belief ebbed away. There is no point of happening, only a moment of departure—unless, like Comrade Kedrov, the finality of self-degradation is achieved. We achieved something less, and I have put down points on the road I traveled —points which marked the line to my departure. I don't know all the bypaths of the road Kantorowicz has traveled since we parted in 1946. We corresponded, many letters at first—and then fewer and fewer as what we could say dried up. And then, from far off, from the Federal Republic of Germany, the voice of Kantorowicz cried out, "I have lost every illusion."

It leaps to mind—"the writer's revolution!"—but it is no revolution we have made now, only the noise that hearts make when they break. Sartre, in his original outburst of hate and horror at the Soviet intervention in Hungary last year, specified that one had to earn the right to denounce communism. Is this all that we have earned through so many years of broken hopes and battered bodies?

When Kantorowicz stood free of Communist power, only days ago, he said, "I have left the area in which the terror of Ulbricht reigns."

Try to comprehend that, not simply this man but the life of this man—if you wish to comprehend the twentieth century. Between his monumental and forlorn dignity and the broken wreck that was Comrade Kedrov at the end

—between the two of them, the tragedy of Communism is delineated. Not the stupid prancing of the cloak-and-dagger boys on the TV screen, not the foolish talk of conspiracies to overthrow the government of the United States by force and violence, not the fevered inventions of the sick minds of professional witnesses—but something so much deeper, so much more terrible, more intimate, more human and more decisive to mankind. What did Kantorowicz leave behind him when he fled from communism? In his statement, he makes muted mention of his thousands of books, his manuscripts, his letters, his notes—all the precious data of the writer as he, the writer, makes his way through this strange and puzzling world. It is the itemization of the refugee; for even the poorest of the poor have a few things, a few sentimentalities, the wrinkled shoe of a first child, a bit of ribbon, a birth certificate, a few pictures, a few books. One is poor but not naked. The refugee is naked.

But other things he left behind resist itemization. I do not know Ulbricht, yet I know him. Not inhuman, like Hitler, but non-human, like Stalin; there is a difference. Hitler turned against the freedom, morality, richness of beauty and culture, and inalienable rights that mankind had won for itself; Stalin simply set it all aside; Ulbricht is righteous, for in his robes of high-priesthood, he serves the altar of the naked god. Somewhere, deep, deep in what is left of his shriveled soul, Ulbricht knows that the god is naked; but he is past the point where the act of knowing can ever make him free. He has lost touch with humankind. For him are no more hopes or visions or high dreams—only the caress of power over his righteousness. It is useless to speculate upon whether he is mad or sane; the important thing is that he is apart from us forever—and equally important that Kantorowicz is not. In his very words, Kantorowicz is tied to us. Who is there who will read this and remain unmoved as Kantorowicz says,

". . . Farewell for a long time to come—if not forever —to friends and fellow workers from the days of common resistance against the Nazi blood terror, to those comrades who—in the firm belief to fight for a just cause—risked their lives with me in the international brigades in Spain—at the fronts of Madrid, Prozoblanco, Teruel and not in the rear headquarters of Albacete, Valencia and Barcelona, comrades who later were fellow prisoners in the concentration camps and prisons. And lastly, I must also take leave of my respected colleagues of the philosophical faculty at the Humboldt University, of my assistants, students, colleagues in scientific and literary work. They all, every one of them, will now be forced to spit after me, to heap abuse on me, to call me a traitor, a renegade and more—only because I am trying to remain true to myself. . . ."

Think a moment of what Kantorowicz is saying. Sartre puts it thus, ". . . I say that man is condemned to be free. Condemned, because he did not create himself, yet, in other respects is free; because once thrown into the world, he is responsible for everything he does."

I do not know whether this is an ultimate truth or whether there is such a thing as an ultimate truth; but it seems to me that it is as much of the truth about the writer as can ever be told. We bear the burden of re-creation. Not as gods do we people our pages, but as chained observers —chained to the reality of the human brotherhood; for when we pick up the pen, we sell our souls, not to the devil, but to the gentle injunction of man. If we do not betray him, he will reward us according to our ability.

I think this holds for all writers. As with other trades, we range from incompetence to genius, but that could not be otherwise. What we do, we do as well as we can, some poorly, some splendidly—but when we evade the responsibility imposed by the nature of our work, we see better than any other the destruction of what talent we possess. Who can yet say what forces drive men to do the work they have learned to do and to do it as best they can? It is part of the whole, vast puzzle of human existence and destiny.

Yet I think that we who have been through this and made the break, clean and sharp, have not come away totally without profit. We have learned something of great importance concerning the manner of our own time, and there is no growth without the pain of learning. So much greater is the agony of those who have not and cannot make this break. We travel through a strange land, but our journey comes to an end. And however disturbing the end of the road may be, there is a special and compensating sweetness in the air one breathes later.

23

In the end, there is fear—the kind of fear that could not possibly exist if the Communist Party were only an organization. It is the deeper, more awful fear of one who has given himself to false gods and given himself too well. When a Communist walks out of the Communist Party, he must travel through a special purgatory that no one other than he who has come through before can possibly understand.

Truly, the simpletons say, "But we have always known the truth about the Party. Why did it take you so long?"

What truth? Even in this brief book, I have put down a picture that few people outside actually understood; and in the Party it is overlaid by a complex of a hundred thousand threads. Earlier I told of the man who cried out against the Russians,

"We Communists taught the world a lesson in how to die with dignity and courage, but when it came our turn to die at the hands of those murderers, they denied us even the small solace of dignity. . . ."

There, in essence, is the complexity of the whole, and if one denies the nobility of the Communist, one can make no sense or reason out of the ignoble horror that the Communist structure begets. Life is just not simple. The American boy from the slums of New York or Chicago who joined the Communist Party, volunteered to fight in Spain against the darkness of fascism, and walked with his still-to-be-fired Springfield into the hell of Jarama Valley—where, as it was said, he learned to die before he learned to fight—was no monster; he was one of the bravest and truest human products of our time.

I feel like pleading for understanding of this point above all else. Let me make this plain in another set of circumstances. I don't know that a documented story has ever been printed in the American press concerning the three thousand Polish Communists who were murdered by the Russian secret police—by the order of Stalin and the men around Stalin. But at least half a dozen Poles of character and reputation have told me this story, and each one of them emphasized the fact that the murdered men were, in their own words, "the cream of our movement, the best and the bravest."

Thus the butcher murders the "best and the bravest" of his own party. It is not simple. Whatever else the Party creates or destroys, it destroys itself within itself, whether by murder, by fear or by mental castration. It takes what is pure and makes it impure. Pledged to reason, it is the ultimate enemy of reason; pledged to progress, it arrives always at stasis.

Therefore it claims immortality, even though it has seen its own honor stained with such a record of the inhumanity of man to man as no previous political party has ever created within itself.

Yet at the basis of Marxism is the premise that only change is certain and eternal. It is the duty of Communists to shatter the mythology and have done with priests and temples and magical ritual, not a duty to their party but to mankind. It is the duty of non-Communists to begin to understand the historical development of the Communist Party.

No force on earth can destroy the Communist Party, but the application of truth will melt it as rain melts salt. Its time is past. The Russian people and the Chinese people are on the brink of such growth and fruition as was never dreamed of in the first decades of this century—even as the whole world stands on the very doorstep of an internationally functioning civilization that can once and for all do away with war and want. Only a fool could imagine that the clique of madmen who—by Khrushchev's own testimony— almost lost the war with Germany are a positive asset in the building of Russian civilization. There is nothing conceivable of creation in the Soviet Union that the Soviet people cannot create, the workers and engineers and scientists and teachers and artists. Rid of the parasitic burden of the Communist Party, given a democratic government upon their socially owned base, they could in short order turn their land into a garden of plenty.

Can we learn that? Only the Russian people can deal with the question of their Communist Party, even as each and every people on earth must deal with the same question; and a Communist Party, any Communist Party, will disappear or destroy its monstrous, monolithic temple structure only when a very significant part of its membership come to understand its functioning nature.

To do this, they must conquer *fear,* for fear of the mysterious and nameless gods of the Party is central to the

Party itself. Nor are we, the United States, exempt from fear; for, under the spell of the "professional patriots," we have taken this shaky edifice of magic ritual and gross superstition and turned it into the unconquerable ogre of our time.

Yet the strength and weakness of the Party are one. No organization based on pseudo-religious cant, cemented with neurotic fear and parading ritualistic magic as a substitute for reason can endure in this second half of the twentieth century. Only the Western nations can make the Communist Party survive. If they succumb to the madness of bellicosity —and it is worth reflecting on the fact that Khrushchev must know that war offers one of the very few possibilities for uniting all factions in Russia behind him—and force the issue, or even allow the issue to proceed to another war, then very likely only the fanatical structure of the Communist Party will survive the holocaust as a functioning organization capable of some sort of rule.

May God help us if this comes to pass! We are at one of those moments in history when the quantitative build-up of social evolution is about to crystallize into new forms and directions. We need to be possessed of deep and abiding faith in that which is close to us, humankind, and we need to have patience. History appears to have spelled out the finish of the time of the Communist Party and perhaps the dawn of socialist democracy and humanism; but only the people of the lands ruled by Communist Parties can decide this issue.

We are poised, I think, between acts of wisdom and acts of destruction. If we act wisely, with a new tolerance, a new understanding and especially a new effort to prove good faith to the people of the East, then it may well be that we will witness the peaceful cooperation of democratic socialism and democratic capitalism in the building of a better world for our children.

24

Unlike other books I have written, this one moved restlessly in the very process of creation; history interlocked with it. It began with a long magazine article, and even before that article saw the light of publication, it was quoted and misquoted—and already I locked horns with men who had once been with me. The book grew in the fury of the conflict and came alive not without an agony that was part of no other writing I had done.

Rumors and bits of news eddied around its creation. When I began it, with the proposition that in the Soviet Union I had been denied both life and death, it was still unknown to Soviet citizens that I had broken hard with the Communist Party. In the course of the writing, a young American college student told hundreds of Soviet people the truth, and there the rumor spread like wildfire—forcing the Soviet leadership to denounce me bitterly in the *Literary Gazette,* the Russian "literary" paper that lays down the line of the Party.

And today, as I write this, the last hope of what will go into this book, news has come, though still unverified, that Ilya Ehrenburg has denounced both Communist rule and Communist literature. Can this be, I ask myself? Can it be that even Ehrenburg, silent in his own fear while they murdered his comrades and colleagues and fellow Jews, has found voice, courage and conscience? So even as I write a tale of horror, nightmare, courage and fear, life parallels the process. Yet withal, so many questions remain unanswered.

Does one leave the Party even as one enters it? What happens, and is it possible ever to convey to an outsider this strange process that even Ehrenburg seems to have shared?

Ten years ago, in 1947, I said to two friends of mine, Communists many more years than I, "Then how does one remain in this movement? How does one go on?"

They had less than sufficient answers, yet the three of us remained for years to come. Here is what happened then. It was during hearings held in Washington by the House Committee on Un-American Activities on the subject of the Communist Party. One of these friends of mine was then the head of the Washington office of the *Daily Worker*. The other was an editor of the paper. I was there as a volunteer background writer, since the hearings were considered important enough by the Party to be covered by three men.

At one point during the hearings, Eugene Dennis appeared as a volunteer witness. He had not then been subpoenaed, but rather offered his presence as a gesture of openness. But openness never came easily to Dennis, and his testimony began and ended with the first question. He was asked his name, and he replied with "Gene Dennis." Then, as a question, a congressman wanted to know whether he had not once had another name. Dennis stood on the ground that under American law Dennis was his legal name and he need answer to no other. The situation became heated, and Dennis was dismissed—and as he walked out, the very large press contingent present deluged him with questions.

As a matter of fact, Dennis had come off very well at

the moment, making a good point out of his right to the name he lived and worked with. I managed to get close to him and tell him that, in my opinion, he had the moral support of every reporter and correspondent in the room. His reaction to this was a blank stare and a desire to know what the devil I was talking about. Dennis was not a very sensitive man, and the whole notion that reporters were anything but his sworn blood enemies at each and every moment of their lives was untenable to him.

He did not talk to the reporters then, but John Gates, who was with him as his aide and press representative, told the reporters that they would hold a press conference in Dennis' hotel suite in about an hour. At that time, Gates said, Dennis would make an announcement of national importance. I am not certain whether or not Gates knew what the announcement would be. We did not—that is, my two friends and myself—nor would Dennis do us the small courtesy of informing us. Dennis was never one to indulge in any sort of equalitarianism with his comrades.

Presently the press conference began, the room packed with the Washington press corps. Fortunately, since so many denials will be flung at this book, Bert Andrews of the New York *Herald-Tribune* made his own shorthand record of the entire conference and printed it in full the following day. It is there for anyone who cares to peruse the whole incredible business. I give only the gist of what followed.

After a number of banalities on the part of Dennis, the press demanded to hear the special break—of promised national importance. Dennis then announced, somewhat ponderously, that he had been in China for several years—a good while ago.

The reporters were dumbfounded. They told Dennis that they did not care whether he had been in China or not. Where was the announcement of national importance? Doggedly, Dennis insisted that the news of his being in China at one time was of national importance. And when the reporters demurred that perhaps his notion of news was different from theirs, Dennis went on the defensive and began to be offensive.

Then someone—I think it was Bert Andrews—asked Dennis who had sent him to China, thinking that this might make some small item. Dennis replied that the *American people* had given him his mission to China.

This incredible nonsense was met with a silence in proportion to its arrogance, and then someone said, "You don't really mean that seriously, do you, Mr. Dennis?" Bert Andrews wanted to know how the American people had assigned him to the mission—by vote? as a diplomat? just how? Dennis then turned his abuse directly on Andrews and began to rant at him as a "paid hireling of the kept press." At which point the other journalists rose in disgust and stalked out of the room, leaving only the three representatives of the *Daily Worker* to hear the rest of the revelation and tirade. But Dennis was not disposed to talk any more for our small readership, and we too got up and left. It was too painful to remain.

We were all three of us sickened and heartbroken at the impossible scene that had just taken place. As Party people, we had to bear the onus of our national leader, and so utterly blasted was our normal process of reasoning that we were unable to talk even to each other.

I remember well how mournfully and slowly we walked

through the streets of Washington. That was when I asked them, older men more experienced in Party life, the question with which I began this unpleasant tale. They had no answers. Was I in the Party, moving closer to it, moving away? I don't know. I asked my two comrades, almost as a rhetorical question,

"What does one do when he is part of a movement the leader of which is either an idiot or a madman?"

Though this story has been told in Communist Party circles for years, it's a horrible story to put into print—and I am fully conscious of that; the horror through the years has been felt by so many of us, and what happens to you in the process is not easy to detail. You have no record of what takes place in the tissues of your mind; it is very complex, and you develop a power of rationalization that is nothing short of incredible. You look at your leaders with contempt and anger, and you say to yourself, "They are not the Party. We are the Party." Antileadership is a political crime in the Party and ground for expulsion, so wise were those who shaped the organization. "There will be other leaders when the time calls for them," said my friend in Washington that night. Always there would be heroic times to call forth grand leadership; and meanwhile we lived through hellish times with the leaders we had.

Who knows what we thought? It was not easy even to admit to ourselves that we wanted to leave, get out of the nightmare. The nightmare specified that whosoever left discarded all hope of salvation. That was not easy to live with. Did one begin to leave the Party when one entered it—does one always? What were the people of Hungary thinking, Communist and non-Communist, when the secret report catalyzed their ideas into action? What would happen today in Russia if *Pravda* printed the full text of the secret report?

I remember that I once prepared a pamphlet. It had drawings in it by some of the finest artists of our time, whom I had persuaded to contribute to it. One in particular, a man of great stature, had drawn a picture of a group of workers. These were all white workers in the picture; but after the pamphlet was printed, fifty thousand copies done and finished, Betty Gannett, a member of the Party secretariat, decided that because the dress of a woman in the picture had blown above her knees, this was an insult to the Negro people. We pleaded that the woman in the picture was a white woman and that dresses do occasionally blow above the knee; but Betty Gannett shrieked at us that the mere possibility that this might be a Negro would offend the entire working class of America. So five thousand dollars' worth of pamphlets were destroyed—five thousand dollars of the hard-saved money that poor people contributed to the Party.

I knew this was madness, frightening insanity—and so did every other Communist concerned. Then consider what was being built up inside of us. I say that something of the same thing has been built up, through the years, in every honest Communist rank-and-filer on earth. I think that all of us began a process of developing horror, hurt, and anger from the day we became members of the Party. Our release was slow, but that was our own agony. I think the world can take comfort in that fact that from here on it will happen more quickly. The sick god was naked from the beginning; there only had to be a voice to proclaim the fact.

25

It would be inconceivable for me to have written the chapters you have just read without doubts. In any attempt to comprehend a situation that has developed historically and to spell it out in such a manner as to promote some understanding of forces and results, the writer is bound to wonder how well he has approximated the reality. Old friends of mine who remained—and still remain—in the Communist Party were willing to forgive me anything I said, so long as I did not publically commit my ideas to paper. They held that the very fact of the Twentieth Congress and the presentation by Khrushchev of the secret report heralded change.

For a full year after the Twentieth Congress of the Russian Communist Party, from February of 1956 to February of 1957,* I waited silently—making no public statement of my changed attitude toward the Communist Party. During that time, I saw the emergence and climb to Kremlin power of Nikita Khrushchev, a leader of a "new type." Not even Stalin, for all his cold-blooded ferocity, had made public

* The actual date of the Twentieth Congress of the Communist Party of the Soviet Union was February 24, 1956. However, the reports of the Congress did not begin to reach the United States until the following month and continued to arrive intermittently until May of 1956. In June of 1956 the Khrushchev secret report, presented at the Congress in February, was made available to the American public for the first time.

display, in diplomatic terms, of boorishness, drunkenness and wild braggadocio; this was new for the Party, if frighteningly familiar in historical terms, this chest-beating, strutting, Jew-hating and Jew-baiting leader of the Communist Party of Russia.

Yet in other ways, he remained true to the Stalinist tradition, the fountainhead of "wisdom," the bottomless pool of ultimate knowledge—which the mantle of Party leadership granted him. It remained for him, for the "new leader" to take in hand and control the "revolution of writers" within Russia, which followed the Twentieth Congress. It also remained for Nikita Khrushchev, in his latest pronouncements on art and the control of art in a Communist state, to put my last doubts to rest.

For while Fadeyev, the then head of the Union of Soviet Writers, had killed himself after Khrushchev's revelations, other writers had plunged into the same heady dance of liberation that we on the *Daily Worker* had experienced. If only briefly, they did taste the wine of freedom at least once, and they began to write in the same measure. I mentioned earlier the book *Not by Bread Alone.* The very fact of this book led me, and many others, to wonder whether perhaps it did not portend significant changes in the literary scene in Russia. But it was not sufficient for literary critics to descend upon the author. The head of state himself had to take a hand, and say of the author:

. . . His book *Not by Bread Alone,* which reactionary forces abroad are now trying to use against us, biasedly scissored out negative facts for tendentious presentation from an unfriendly angle. Dudintsev's book has, true, pages rightly and strongly written, but its general trend is wrong at the root of it. The reader gets the impression that its author is not concerned for having the shortcomings he sees in our life removed, that he deliberately lays on the colors thick and rubs his hands in malicious glee over these shortcomings. This approach to the presentation of reality in works of literature and art is nothing but a craving to misrepresent it as through a crooked mirror.

The meaning of such a pronouncement far transcends the worn and tired ideas, presented in the shoddy language that a thousand Communist leaders have used to say more or less the same thing. In practical fact, Khrushchev is saying, *"We will tolerate no more such books."*

It is there, in essence, that the tragedy lies. People have said to me, in great aggravation, "Suppose you as a writer do have to give up some of your precious freedom? Suppose we even have to dispense with great literature, as you call it? Isn't that a very small sacrifice in the light of the mighty forward march of all mankind toward socialism?"

If anything is dangerous sophistry, this kind of reasoning is; for not only is the cart before the horse but both are turned upside-down. A nonexistent goal—in any terms understandable to those who cherish socialism—is used to justify the most tyrannical means; and for the first time in all of its existence, human society is presented with the spectacle of great masses of plain people pledged to the contraction of freedom. Yet the method is not new; it was

Adolf Hitler who expounded on the value of the monumental lie, and in the same speech to writers quoted above,
Nikita Khrushchev said,

> The strength of Soviet society lies in that the Com-
> munist Party and people are one. . . .

Many people might view this statement with suspicion
and doubt, but only one who has spent the years of his adult
life in the Communist movement can completely comprehend how utterly outrageous and incredible it is. The Communist Party and the people are not one—and millions of
Communists know that Khrushchev lies. I think I have
proved in the material presented here that the Party itself
is not one, but a merciless situation of stress between membership and leadership—a situation that can only be maintained by a bloody repression of any and all dissent. How
much more terrible and unbearable then must be the contradiction between the Communist Party and the people
of any country where it has power! How shameless, how
utterly shameless this statement of Khrushchev is!

And as for his attitude toward writers—and thereby the
official Communist attitude toward writers—he spells it out
in unmistakable terms, again in the same recent address to
the writers of the Soviet Union:

> Unfortunately, among literary and art workers, there
> are people, advocates of "freedom of creation," who
> want that we . . . should not criticize such works which
> distortedly portray the life of Soviet society. To these
> people, it appears, the guidance of literature and art

by the Party and the state is oppressive. They oppose this guidance, sometimes directly, but more often they conceal their moods and desires by talk about excessive tutelage, fettering of initiative, etc. We openly declare that such views run counter to the Leninist principles of the Party's and the state's attitude to the questions of literature and art.

So there it is—the official pronouncement a year and a half after the "secret" speech; and there is the new freedom which Russia has granted to its writers.

How little has changed! In 1954, Soviet representatives told me fervently that never again would one man rule their country; but we have seen the return of a single man to power. The whole world has watched his brutal and thoroughly Stalinist climb to power. Under the world's scrutiny, he appears to have refrained from the callous murder of his defeated colleagues that was the mode of Stalin's time; instead, he publicly exercised a grotesque sense of humor, if this sort of thing can be called humor.

World figures such as Molotov, Malenkov and Shepilov were sent into ignominious exile, even as the Roman emperors delivered their palace enemies to the barbarian borders of their realm. And grinning and cackling, Mr. Nikita Khrushchev paraded his victory and himself before the world, the symbol of "all man's hope."

I wonder how those *Pravda* writers who spoke with such love and admiration of Shepilov—he was then editor of *Pravda*—feel today? In their world, their feelings must remain unknown. They have received their orders—to take their pens in hand and write their "odes to the Russian people."

183

I wonder what odes they would write if the hangman's hands were tied? I knew a number of Russian writers, many personally, more through correspondence. I knew them as human beings, people of warmth and dignity, and I agree with Mr. Khrushchev that such people are dangerous. But perhaps he does not know how dangerous they actually are. It is the essence of Mr. Khrushchev's thinking that he has at best a poor knowledge of people. Hangmen cannot be unduly concerned with the hopes and needs of people; it is not in the nature of their trade. Yet hangmen learn to fear people.

It was an American poet who wrote that "the mills of God grind slowly, yet they grind exceeding small."

But perhaps, as I noted before, the warning is ours as well. It is dangerous to hear all voices, but even more dangerous to stifle a single one. What a price mankind has paid to learn this!

Nor, in our own age of conformity, can we consider the price with any degree of comfort or smugness. It is worth remembering that the writer did not simply happen; he is not a happenstance nuisance, a sort of universal North Jersey mosquito—existing for no other purpose than to annoy, discomfort and provoke. Nor is he a paid entertainer whose sole mission is to weave the cloth that the dream-factory produces. He is a part—a very necessary part—of the strange and exciting logic of social development, and it is as a gadfly, critic and social castigator that he has made perhaps his most significant contribution to the evolution of civilization.

On either side of the fence, the injunction toward conformity is both reactionary and despicable. The gross vulgarity, the sentimental and dangerous nonsense of Khrushchev's "advice" to Russian writers is not a literary limitation per se; it becomes most damaging as a *total* distortion of thinking, and it is precisely this *total* distortion that the writer experiences within the Communist movement. What you have just read in this book was a part of my own experience when I decided to leave the Communist Party. It was on the basis of this experience that I wrote to certain friends in the Soviet Union and told them directly about the decision I had come to.

These friends were writers, whose acquaintance I had made through years of correspondence; and with some justification, I had the feeling that they shared certain deep-founded beliefs and principles that were part of my own thought and action, a feeling for the individual and a love of equalitarianism that went beyond any Party affiliation. In particular, I felt this to be the case with Boris Polovoy, in spite of the grotesque and unexplainable invention about Kvitko—so like Fadeyev's earlier inventions. I put forward the question of whether we had a relationship of value as human beings deeply interested in the problems of our times.

It was most important to attempt to see this through with Polovoy, for as the head of the Union of Soviet Writers, he would, so to speak, set a political as well as a moral tone. I was not simply approaching him as a friend and a writer—but as a writer who had once been a Communist and now no longer was. At the same time, I wrote to Boris Isakov, the head of the Foreign Commission of the Union of Soviet Writers; and, perhaps with undue provocation, said that I hoped fear would not prevent him from replying to my letter. It is to this statement that Boris Polovoy refers in his letter to me, which follows. I print this letter in full, because I feel that it demonstrates in all complexity the nature of the problems I have set forth in this book. It reached me in March, 1957—I believe on the 25th, the same day on which I answered it. This was seven weeks after I had written to Polovoy to inform him of my own action. His letter follows:

DEAR HOWARD:

You see, I am writing to you and without a shade of the fear you have hinted at in your letter to our mutual friend Isakov. By the way, he did not deserve to be hurt by you in this way. You are too much of an artist not to understand that there is little point in taking such a tone with friends.

I confess I was deeply grieved to hear of your decision. We have met only once, but we have corresponded for a long time, and I for one have always looked forward eagerly to your letters. From them, and from your books, too, of course, I have formed for myself a picture of a man who all his life has rowed against the current and sacrificed a great deal for the sake of a lofty goal. And in our literary discussions I often point to you as an inspiring example of true courage and stanch conviction.

Hence the latest news about you came to me as a great shock. The more so that I learned about it not from a friendly letter from you or from one of the small but courageous publications you have been associated with for so many years, but from one of the organs of the big, rich and noisy press and, moreover, from an interview granted a man I cannot respect as a journalist. Thus, this news was for me especially bitter.

I am an old soldier and my nerves are pretty strong. But that night I could not fall asleep. I kept thinking of your books. Their heroes crowded around me and together with them, as it were, I went over the whole situation. I felt sure that Gideon Jackson, who fought the good fight to the bitter end, would not have been less taken aback than I was by what had happened. Neither would Spartacus, even if he did live at a time when there were neither the philosophical theories nor the practical experience that throw light over mankind's path today, a time without the cultural values of today or the progressive intellectuals bearing aloft the banner of peace at all circumstances. You, of course, know your Spartacus better than I, but I feel sure that, had he been with me that night he would not have been any less distressed and perplexed than I. Or George Washington, the man I looked up to in my childhood and whom I rediscovered in your book; in like circumstances he surely would have said: "No matter how hard the battle, I must hold out today in order to win tomorrow!" As for Silas Timberman, logic tells me that, although he would find things just as hard as you, he nevertheless would actively disagree with your decision.

It is said that an author invests some particle of himself in his heroes. For this reason alone your heroes, whom millions have come to love, would, for all their grit and stamina, be disturbed if they could hear what the lugubrious well-known radio voice has been saying by air for Russia, allegedly on your authority. Incidentally, its aim is clear to me. They are trying to destroy the popularity of your books among 900,000,000 readers and that of yourself, as well. However, your friends know how much the unscrupulous ravings of the Voice are worth; we do not believe that you would try to justify your latest step which in itself is your private affair, of course, by renouncing in terms as violent as the Voice would have it everything you have accepted, championed and defended in your books, public speeches and letters only yesterday.

Vercors, the chairman of the French Writers' National Committee, was here recently. You know him, of course, if only from his books and articles. He was very prominent in the French Resistance, a gifted artist and very far from communism in his political views. He came to see me and we spent a whole evening and a good part of the night talking. We emptied several pots of coffee in the process. Julia finally gave up and went to bed, but we were still hard at it. Of course we did not agree on a great many points, but we remained friends, because we both felt that the main thing now is to strengthen ties between writers of East and West, and that this can be accomplished not by quibbling and mutual recriminations—which only gives everyone concerned a headache and provides malicious pleasure to the outsiders—but by calm cool-headed interchange of views. And, of course, we found common ground on the principal issue, Peace, which is equally essential to East and West, to Rights and Lefts, to Catholics like Vercors and to atheists like myself.

I recall this visit of Vercors', my dear Howard, because I want to say this. Many of my writer friends are not Communists, some indeed belong to what I consider reactionary parties. Different outlooks on life, different ideas about the future, however, do not prevent us from corresponding, visiting one another and exchanging views on life and literature. But among these friends of mine there is not a single one who adds fuel to the fire of the cold war.

I know you will understand me and share my feelings in this respect. I remember with what love and pride you spoke of your fellow countrymen that time we met and how indignant you were about newspaper men who thoughtlessly and groundlessly disparage all that your people hold sacred, belittle their achievements and offend their national pride and the Stars and Stripes. I fully shared your sentiments and quoted them in my "American Diaries." For my part I have done my best in that book not to offend the American reader in any way by hasty judgments or superficial opinions. Incidentally, I sent you a copy of it long ago so if you wish you can judge for yourself. I think, Howard, I am entitled therefore to expect similar consideration from you.

As for your books, all the efforts of the Voice have not damaged them. Our magazines and book publishers continue to bring them to the reading public, adults and children. In particular, "Lola Gregg," which has just appeared in Russian, as I wrote you in my letter of February 15, which you probably already have received, is beginning to win the hearts of its readers.

Well, dear Howard, that is how things stand. I shall continue to look forward with impatience to your letters for I firmly believe that we both of us—yes, both of us, I am sure of it—have much in common to do in the precious fight for peace and progress. Yes, I am very hopeful of this—even of work in common.

We are both family men. You have two children, I have three. Really—devil take it—is not that in itself a common platform on which to work together for peace —peace for them? Eh, old man, how good it would be for us to get together over a glass of vodka or whisky —it makes no difference which—and after the old custom of the intelligentsia talk and argue late into the night, regardless of the yawns and angry glances of the wife. But I wouldn't be allowed inside the U.S. and you wouldn't be allowed outside it.

But I really have rambled on this time! I had better stop before this letter becomes too heavy to be airmailed. To dear Bette, best regards from me and from Julia —nothing has changed in their relations, at least, although they have never actually met. But, then, wives are always wiser than husbands.

18 March 1957   Yours sincerely,
BORIS POLOVOY

P. S. I think I shall cable you simultaneously with this letter because it looks as if the post has become sluggish and my last letter to you, sent in mid-February, evidently has not yet reached you.

Such was Polovoy's reply to a series of deeply important questions which I had directed to him. On the day I received his letter, I answered him as follows:

DEAR BORIS:

To hear from you was good, believe me. Your letter came today, and I read it hungrily; and I felt the warmth and happiness of hearing your voice again, for I hear it in any letter of yours. You and Isakov I treasure as friends, as Bette does; this must not change.

But if only in your letter you had answered some of our questions! It's neither important nor significant that the Voice of America makes capital of my action. I assure you they made much greater capital of Khrushchev's "secret speech," and one cannot silence any and all criticism with the protest that the Voice of America will use it.

I raised questions, points of heartbreaking life and death significance; are there no answers? Are we children or fools that our pleading insistence for some explanations is always to be met with rhetoric? Can it do more harm than has already been done to tell us why Jewish writers were murdered by your Government, why Bulganin uses anti-Semitism as foreign policy, why a whole disgraceful theory of anti-Semitism was born and used in your land under the foolish name of "cosmopolitanism"?

Is it beyond the power of your Government or yourself to tell us something more sensible in explanation of the unprecedented orgy of murder under Stalin than such nonsense as "the cult of the individual"? We are told that Beria stood up against Stalin, opposed Stalin's madness and was murdered by Khrushchev and others because he had the facts of their crimes. Why isn't this refuted? Why are not these rumors put to rest? Where are the minutes of Beria's trial?

Why don't we hear your voice, Isakov's, and other voices in defense of the book "Not by Bread Alone"? Perhaps the book is worthless; must not the writer be defended? Why will no one tell us how Itzik Feffer died? The Poles informed us that Khrushchev attempted to use anti-Semitism to sway the inner struggle in Poland. Why does no one deny this? Where is one little word of the criticism and self-criticism we have been hearing so much about?

Why did Pravda try to sway the inner struggle of the party here, supporting Foster and the men around him? These are not good men. They are men who are divorced from every reality in our land. The best, the bravest in the party here are ranged against them.

And what of your own letter, Boris? Why must you indulge in such nonsense as the "post becoming slow indeed"? For the past year, there has been hardly a day when I did not receive one or two letters from Russia. All sorts of people wrote to me—school children, workers, teachers, editors, theatre people—and, of course, you and your colleagues. How was it then that, three days after the announcement in The New York Times that I had left the Communist party, all my mail from Russia abruptly ceased?

You know as well as I do that then there was no mention of my action in the Soviet press. Yet not one letter got through. Obviously all letters to me were stopped in the post office—just as your earlier letter to me was stopped in the post office. Is this freedom—or even common sense? For all you say about the United States, I have been writing to Russia for years and receiving mail from Russia, too, and none of it has ever been stopped because of anything I said or did.

Why do these things go on?

Can no one leave the Communist party honestly and openly, criticize Soviet leadership honestly and openly, and still be treated as a part of mankind? Your own letter says that you still regard me as a friend, in spite of what I have done—intimating that I have done something dishonorable and tragic.

But has it ever been dishonorable to follow the dictates of one's own conscience? There are millions of good and honorable people in the world who feel as I do and who are asking the same questions I ask. Are you going to win them with the kind of argument you put forth in your letter? You speak of Vercors, whom I also respect. But Vercors was not a Communist; he did not put his life and his honor as a seal on the actions of the Soviet Union. I did, and that makes a difference, if you will only think about it.

If you see this only in terms of myself, you and your colleagues will learn nothing. I am not the first intellectual to leave the party here since the news of the "Khrushchev report." [four names deleted by author] are only a few of the many who left already. And with them went hundreds of workers and other party people, good, honest, clear-thinking people whom I honor and respect.

Last summer, Boris, I received a cable from Radio Moscow, asking for my views on testing the atom bomb. I replied that all nations should stop testing it, but that the Soviet Union, as a Socialist nation dedicated to mankind, should lead this. I said that the Soviet Union must stop now, whether or not the others agree. I may have been wrong, but this was my opinion. Why was it never used? Why did I get no reply? What kind of childish pretense is that that any ideas you find distasteful can be quietly buried? Wasn't this the same thing as the idiotic deletion of Gene Dennis' comment on the destruction of Jewish culture—when the rest of his speech was printed in Pravda?

And why—why, Boris, did you tell us here in New York that the Yiddish writer, Kvitko, was alive and well and living in your apartment house as your neighbor, when he was among those executed and long since dead? Why? Why did you have to lie? Why could you not avoid the question and tell us you did not know or would not discuss it? Why did you lie in so awful and deliberate a manner?

By now you have my statement in Mainstream. Publish it. Publish this letter. Answer my arguments. Tell me that terror is gone. Tell me that anti-Semitism is over and done with. Demand an end to capital punishment—the old and fine dream of socialism. Tell us the truth—only that, the truth. I may have been a fool not to have known of this terror before, but I did not know.

Do you want me to worship the Communist party as an icon? Believe me, I worship something better—truth and freedom, and how can you ask that one tyranny be traded for another?

I ventured my life and fortune to speak the truth as I saw it. Will you? Print this in The Literary Gazette. Open the doors! Let the words fly! Only in that way can the world-hurt be healed. And let no man suffer for speaking his mind forthrightly and honestly.

And I want to remain your friend. Can I? It is up to you.

HOWARD FAST

At this point, I think, we have a clear and balanced—or at least to the very best of my ability—picture of the writer and the Communist Party; not in full, certainly, but in part— and no book can present more than a significant part of any question. Nikita Khrushchev's firm injunction to Soviet writers looms heavily—"the portrayal of a bright future with the Communist Party as its guiding sun."

The friendship I asked for has been answered with silence, for from the time I wrote the letter until today, no word has come from Polovoy. Did I slander him? There were many witnesses, all of them Communists, to his rationale of Kvitko; is it slander to state that Kvitko was dead when Polovoy spoke? Or is there an explanation as to why men do what they do?

Even through the difficult years I spent in the Communist Party, I clung to the premise that I was a rational human being. I asked for the facts; and if I was loath to believe them as presented by the enemies of the Soviet Union, I perforce had to believe them when they were presented by the Communist Party itself. At that point, I faced the necessity of understanding what had happened to me and to my comrades —and of being able to communicate that understanding to others who were not Communists. To that point, I have written this book.

But having done so, and having put down my thinking, it would surely be irrational at this point to pretend that I consider the Communist Party an organization which can benefit mankind. Quite the reverse. Is this then the difference between myself and Vercors, as seen in the mind of Polovoy? Is the Party the premise for all his thoughts and actions? If so, then my final question to him was as rhetorical in consequence as the tragically meaningful questions which I put into my letter. It may very well be that Polovoy considers himself a "free man," but even if he does, he also accepts the definition of that "freedom" within the taboo and punishment of the Communist Party.

That it is a sort of freedom, I will not deny. When I was a prisoner in jail, I also had freedom of a sort, even if it was only the freedom to pace in a cell. When I was taken out of that cell and brought to another Federal prison, I had a larger degree of freedom; but not even the most bemused prison guard would have claimed that my freedom matched the broadest freedom that civilization has obtained for mankind.

I can only speculate on why—in the narrow sense—my letter to Polovoy was not answered. In a broader sense, I know why it was not answered; and though Communist writers, inside and outside of the Soviet Union, may deride and "explain" my words as the words of one they are now duty bound to characterize with every foul name in their lexicon—they also know, very truly, very deeply, why my letter was not answered.

It is because I have found freedom, and they have not. Not because the United States of America is a perfect democracy—its history of imperfection has filled many a book and will continue to do so—but because it is a land where the individual, in his work and in his rights, is recognized and defended. Sometimes better, sometimes worse—but always defended.

Neither Nikita Khrushchev nor Boris Polovoy has earned the right to speak of the "bright future" of mankind; for if history has taught us one certain lesson, it is this: that where the individual is degraded, oppressed and controlled by fear—whether in name of king or church or party or state —the future is not bright but dark and foreboding indeed.

Whatever the Communist Party once was, today it is a prison for man's best and boldest dreams. Tomorrow belongs to those who break down the prison walls that enclose the minds of men, not to those who support such walls. For mankind, the promise of tomorrow always has been and always will be the widening of intellect and horizon—in ever greater vistas of individual freedom.